大唐丝路

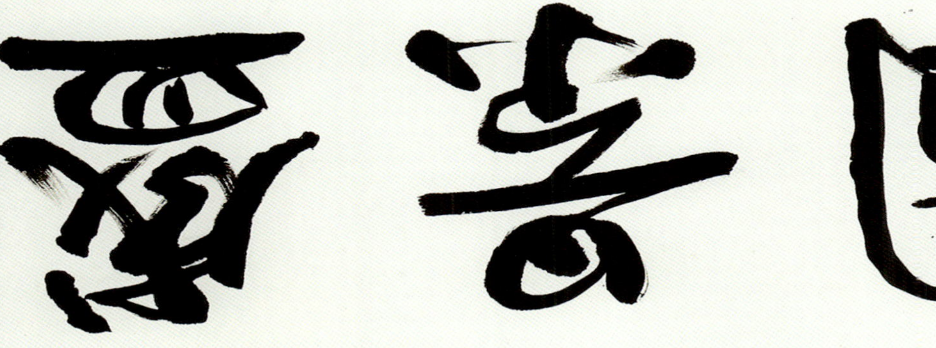

中東印度中國和歐洲這四大地區肥沃的江河流域及平原孕育了世界歷史上最為偉大的中國文明古巴比倫文明古希臘文明以及古埃及文明和古印度文明這五大文明使歐亞大陸成為了在世界歷史發展中起着重大作用的核心地區古中國文明是以黃河流域和長江流域為中心而發展起來的她是世界五大文明中唯一倖存的古國文明中華文明其所以能延續至今是因為中國人強調的是天人合一的哲學理念一直以來都在遵循着和諧包容的和而不同的處世原則中華民族從來就是一個愛好和平在進求物質文明的同時從未放棄過精神幸福進求的偉大民族從西漢張騫開闢的陸上絲綢之路到唐朝宦官楊良瑤首次下西洋所開創的海上絲綢之路以來中華民族都是以和平傳播先進文明和探索經濟交流為目的的友好出訪西漢昔期漢武帝派遣了由張騫帶隊的使節出使西域從此便開闢了以長安為起點經由甘肅新疆到中亞西亞後來並聯接了地中海各國的一條陸上交流往來的商業通道十九世紀下半期德國地理學家費迪南馮李希霍芬在他出版的中國一書中稱之為絲綢之路中國是絲綢的故鄉在經由這條路線進行的貿易商品中中國的絲綢最具代表性故稱之為絲綢之路絲綢之路是歷史上橫貫歐亞大陸的世

界貿易交流主道其基本走向定於兩漢時期包括南道中道北道三條主要線路北方陸上絲路指由黃河中下游通達西域的商路包括草原森林絲路沙和漠綠洲絲路沙漠綠洲絲路其延續千餘年之久沿線文物遺存甚多是絲路的主幹道草原森林絲路是從黃河中游北上穿蒙古高原越西伯利亞平原南部至中亞分兩支一支西南行達波斯轉西行另一支西行翻拉爾山越伏爾加河抵黑海濱兩路在西亞輻合抵地中海沿岸國家沙漠綠洲絲路這條主要幹道其全長七千多公里分東中西三段東段自長安至敦煌較之中西段相對穩定但洛陽長安以西又分三線其北線由長安東漢時由洛陽沿渭河至虢縣即今寶雞過汧縣即今隴縣越六盤山固原和海原沿祖厲河在靖遠渡黃河至姑臧即今武威路程較短沿途供給條件亦差是早期的主要路線南線由長安東漢昔由洛陽沿渭河過隴關上邽即今天水狄道即今臨洮枹罕即今河洲由永靖渡黃河穿西寧越大門拔穀即今偏都口至張掖中線與南線在上邽分道過隴山至金城郡即今蘭州渡黃河溯莊浪河翻烏鞘嶺至姑臧南線補給條件雖好但遠道較長因此中線後來成為主要幹線南北中三線會合後由張掖經酒泉瓜州至敦煌中段是敦煌至蔥嶺今帕米爾或怛羅斯即今江布尔自玉門關陽關出西

域有兩道其一是從鄯善傍南山北波河西行至莎車為南道南道西逾蔥嶺則出大月氏安息其二是自車師前王庭即今吐魯番隨北山波河西行至疏勒即今喀什為北道北道西逾蔥嶺則出大宛康居奄蔡即黑海鹹海間北道上有兩條重要岔道一是由焉耆西南行穿塔克拉瑪幹沙漠至南道的於闐一是從龜茲即今庫車西行過姑墨阿克蘇溫宿烏什翻拔達嶺即別疊裏山口經赤穀城即烏孫首府西行至怛羅斯由於南北兩道穿行在白龍堆哈拉順和塔克拉瑪幹大沙漠條件惡劣道路艱難東漢昔在北道之北另開一道隋唐時成為一條重要通衢稱新北道原來的漢北衢改稱中衢新北道由敦煌西北行經伊吾即哈密蒲類海即今巴裏坤湖北庭即吉木薩爾輪臺即米泉弓月城即霍城碎葉即托克瑪克至怛羅斯西段蔥嶺至羅馬絲路西段涉及範圍較廣包括中亞南亞西亞和歐洲歷史上的國家眾多民族關係複雜因而路線常有變化大體可分為南中北三道南道由蔥嶺西行越興都庫什山至阿富汗喀布爾後分兩路一西行至赫拉特與經蘭氏城而來的中道相會再西行穿巴格達大馬士革抵地中海東岸西頓或貝魯特由海路轉至羅馬另一線從白沙瓦南

也分兩支一經鈸汗即今貴爾斡納康即今撒馬爾罕安即今布哈拉至木鹿與中道會西行一經恒羅斯沿錫爾河西北行繞過鹹海裏海北岸至亞速海東岸的墖那由水路轉刻赤抵君士坦丁堡即今伊斯坦布爾其他除了上述的路線之外在唐朝又派遣使臣楊良瑤率領使團航海出使黑衣大食六百多年後明成祖永樂三年又派遣太監鄭和七次率船隊遠航印度洋西岸由此海上絲綢之路的誕生以及後來出現的南線絲綢之路對中國和阿拉伯世界的政治經濟和文化交往又作出了非常重要巨大的貢獻海上絲路起於秦漢興於隋唐盛於宋元明初達到頂峰明中葉因海禁而衰落海上絲路的重要起點有番禺後改稱廣州登州即今煙臺揚州明州泉州劉家港等規模最大的港口是廣州和泉州歷代海上絲路亦可分三大航線東洋航線由中國沿海港至朝鮮日本南洋航線由中國沿海港至東南亞諸國西洋航線由中國沿海港至南亞阿拉伯和東非沿海諸國從張騫首次西域之行到絲綢之路的蓬勃發展中國人從來都是懷揣幸福夢想滿懷熱情的把自己創造的物質及精神文明的偉大成果拿來與世界人民所共用這些文明成果中既包括中國的絲綢茶葉瓷器等生產技術及產品也包括四大發明的偉大科技成果和諸子百家的經典學說理念這些中華民族的文明成果通過絲綢之路得以廣泛傳播和推廣為推進世界文明的延續與發展做出了非常卓越的貢獻今天我們一如既往地踏著祖先的足迹要在中華民族再次崛起的同時把我們物質文明的發展成果和歷史文明的精神財富拿出來與世界各族人民共同分享一種文明的延續不僅是一個國家和民族的精神血脈的延續既要薪火相傳代代守護更需要與時俱進勇於創新的不懈追求我們為了把中國這箇偉大文明古國曾經輝煌的歷史展現出來以勵我們今天能夠在習近平主席的倡導和引領下更好的完成新時期絲綢之路的歷史使命利用絲綢之路這個傳統的金色紐帶讓世界人民共同分享中華民族這箇偉大古國文明的思想智慧和中國日益強盛的經濟科技文明成果我們採用了先進的現代媒介手段要讓收藏在博物館裏的文物動起來讓書寫在古籍裏的故事活起來本次金色絲路盛世輝煌中華文明全球行繪畫展就是採用了聲光電全新的展覽形式集中展示了絲綢之路的起源和發展以及與之有關的歷史人物與經典故事大唐絲路盛景圖就是以氣勢恢宏的長卷形式用富麗堂皇的工筆畫手法真實的再現了大唐盛世時期中國古絲綢之路起點上的繁榮景象中國五千年的輝煌文明是在儒釋道三家文化思想背景下協調發展起來的在世界五大文明中她其所以能延續至今是與中華民族善於吸納世界先進文化的優良品質密不可分的中國人民在和世界各民族人民進行友好往來中總會海納百川式的吸收有益文化並予以發展佛教能在中國得以發揚光大就是很好的例證自東漢明帝永平年間由印度梵僧迦葉摩騰攜經來華並翻譯成四十二章佛經以後從東漢至魏晉南北朝五百年間大量佛典被翻譯成漢文經書這些佛經通過幾代祖師大德的弘講注疏終於發展出隋唐諸代宗派林立的佛傳盛象本長卷就是以草堂寺為背景描繪出了大唐盛世時期的絲綢之路在這裏的繁華景象草堂寺是佛教三輪宗祖鳩摩羅什譯經之聖地它被佛教三輪宗華嚴宗和日蓮宗尊奉為祖庭斯長卷描繪的就是草堂寺廟市中各種交易活動場面以及唐玄奘在草堂寺俗堂講經時的真實場面生動的再現了當時在這裏發生過的絲路繁榮盛況畫面中不但對商旅相繼職貢不絕的絲路繁壯場面進行了精心刻畫也對廟市中的善男信女販夫走卒以及雜玩百技的市井生活進行了生動描繪真實再現了唐代詩人韓愈所描述的街東街西講佛經撞鐘吹螺鬧宮廷的市井繁榮盛況

歲在丙申之年

雷珍民奉書於漢唐古都長安

佛

佛
什法師像

樂

蒸餅

大唐丝路盛景图

Magnificent View of the Silk Road in Great Tang Dynasty

主编：吴铭峰
绘画：雒建安、邓先荷

目录
Catalog

前言

中国与西方文化交流源远流长。作为横贯东西、连接欧亚的交通路线，丝绸之路萌发于贸易的自发往来。公元前二世纪晚期，西汉张骞在西域，开通举世闻名的丝绸之路，中西之间的文化交流进入新世纪。丝绸之路是当时世界上东西方之间最重要的贸易和文化交流通道，历经发展而内涵不断扩展，形成了以绿洲、草原和海上三大干线为主的网状交通系统，并在唐代达到鼎盛，有力地促进各国之间政治、经济和文化交流，创造出古代世界灿烂文明。

两千余年来，丝绸之路作为中国交通大动脉，承载着中国与世界的交往与对话，引动世界文明发展，成为不同文化相互交流与合作的精神象征，为当今世界和平与发展提供了价值典范。

昔日丝绸之路，今日更加辉煌。2013年，国家主席习近平提出了共建“一带一路”的伟大倡议，指出“‘一带一路’建设秉持的是共商、共建、共享原则，不是封闭的，而是开放包容的；不是中国一家独唱，而是沿线国家的合唱。”“不论是发展经济、改善民生，还是应对危机、加快调整，许多沿线国家同我国有着共同利益。”“我们欢迎周边国家参与到合作中来，共同推进‘一带一路’建设，携手实现和平、发展、合作的愿景。”这更加大大促进丝路精神和价值的弘扬和传播，犹如大鹏展翅，有力推动中华民族的伟大腾飞，也更带动世界各国比翼齐飞。

《金色丝路——一带一路中华文化全球行》国画油画展，是为配合中国文化部和陕西省人民政府联合主办的“中华人民共和国第三届国际丝路艺术节—文化全球行”活动而举办。旨在展示丝绸之路的历史过往与灿烂成就，宣扬其时代精神和历史价值，提倡平等、友好、包容、交流、互鉴的发展理念，为实现习近平总书记“一带一路”伟大倡议做出贡献。

这些国画油画以独特的创意、精美的工笔描绘了丝绸之路孤烟大漠、血色残阳，万水千山、流沙飞扬自然风情中的经典传闻、人物典型、名胜古迹，以及佛经盛传、文化交流、商品贸易的繁荣景象。绘画构思细腻、寓意深刻、内容丰富、气势宏伟，历史跨度大，人物表情生动活泼，是对丝绸之路精神和价值的生动写照和真实展示，是丝绸之路历史风貌的真实再现，对于弘扬丝路精神，加快“一带一路”建设，实现习近平总书记“一带一路”伟大愿景，具有十分重要的历史和现实意义。

Preface

China has a long history of cultural exchanges with the west. As the transportation line traversing the east and the west, the Silk Road developed from spontaneous trade. In the late second century B. C, Zhang Qian was ordered to go to the West Regimes, opened up the well-known Silk Road. Cultural exchanges between China and the West stepped into the new century. The Silk Road was the most important trade and cultural exchange channel between the East and the West in the world. It has formed a transport system consisted of three main lines: oasis line, grassland line and sea line, and reached its peak in the Tang Dynasty. The Silk Road has promoted political, economic and cultural exchanges among countries, and created a splendid civilization of ancient world.

The Silk Road was Chinese transportation artery; it took the mission of exchanges and dialogues with the world, motivated the development of world civilization over the past two thousand years, and became the spiritual symbol of the communication and cooperation among different cultures. It provided a valuable example of peace and development for the modern world.

Nowadays, the Silk Road has become much more brilliant. In 2003, President Xi Jinping raised the initiative of "the Belt and Road", which should be jointly built through consultation to meet the interests of all. It is not closed, but open and inclusive. It is not a solo, but chorus. We have common ideals and pursuit of developing economic, improving people's livelihood, responding to the crisis, and speeding up the adjustment. It is open to all the countries, jointly promote the "The Belt and Road 'construction, work together to achieve peace, development and cooperation. It will greatly promote the development and dissemination of the spirit and value of the Silk Road. And it will also promote the rise of the Chinese nation, drive the whole world fly.

Exhibition of traditional Chinese painting —— "The golden Silk Road - Belt and Road Initiative for global Chinese culture" was held with "the Third International Silk Road Art Festival - culture globalization", which organized by Culture Ministry of China and the People's Government of Shaanxi Province. It aims to show the history and brilliant achievements of the Silk Road, promote the spirit of the times and historical value, advocate the idea of equality, friendship, tolerance, communication and mutual learning, and contribute to implement the great initiative of "the Belt and Road".

These paintings describe the desert solitary smoke, red sun on the Silk Road with unique creative and exquisite fine brushwork. They are exquisite, profound, rich and magnificent. It is a vivid portrayal of the spirit and value of the Silk Road and shows the real history of the Silk Road. The exhibition will propagate the spirit of the Silk Road, speed up the "The Belt and Road" construction, and implement the great initiative of "the Belt and Road".

陆上丝绸之路

Land Silk Road

陆上丝绸之路 Land Silk Road

丝绸之路概述

欧亚大陆这片神奇的土地，孕育了世界历史上最为伟大的古中国文明、古巴比伦文明、古希腊文明、古埃及文明和古印度文明。这古老而优秀的五大文明也使得欧亚大陆成为了世界历史发展进程中起重大作用的核心地区。而古中国文明则是这五大文明当中，迄今为止还在生机勃勃地发展着，并且对历史仍然起着巨大推动作用的唯一幸存的古国文明。

中华文明之所以能延续至今，是因为中国人强调天人合一的哲学理念，一直以来都遵循着和谐包容的和而不同的处世原则。中华民族从来就是一个爱好和平，在追求物质文明的同时从未放弃过精神幸福追求的伟大民族，他们勇于探索外部的世界，并且在探寻未知的道路上始终保持着友善而包容的心态。西汉时期汉武帝派遣使臣张骞带队出使西域，从此开辟了以长安为起点，经由甘肃新疆到中亚西亚，并联接了地中海各国的一条陆上交流往来的商业通道；十九世纪下半期德国地理学家费迪南·冯·李希霍芬在他出版的《中国》一书中称之为“丝绸之路”，因为中国是丝绸的故乡，在经由这条路线进行的贸易中，中国输出的大量商品丝绸是最具代表性的。后来，史学家把沟通中西方的商路统称丝绸之路。因其上下跨越历史 2000 多年，涉及陆路与海路，所以按历史划分有先秦、汉唐、宋元、明清 4 个时期，按线路划分又有陆上丝路与海上丝路之别。在唐朝中期以前，中国对外主通道是陆上丝绸之路，之后由于战乱及经济重心转移等原因，“海上丝绸之路”逐渐取代陆路成为中外贸易交流主通道，在宋元时期成为了范围覆盖大半个地球的人类历史活动和东西方文化经济交流的重要载体。实际上，海上丝绸之路的雏形在秦汉时期便已存在，经过魏晋的发展，隋唐的繁盛，直到宋元时期到达顶峰。无论是陆上丝绸之路还是海上丝绸之路，它们所反映的，都是古代中国人民积极寻求与外界的交流，向往和平与沟通，勇于探索和冒险的美好精神。

“陆上丝绸之路”

丝绸之路，始于古代中国，是连接亚洲、非洲和欧洲的古代路上商业贸易路线，又被称为石之路、佛教之路、香料之路。“陆上丝绸之路”是连接中国腹地与欧洲诸地的陆上商业贸易通道，形成于公元前 2 世纪与公元 1 世纪间，直至 16 世纪仍保留使用，是一条东方与西方之间经济、政治、文化进行交流的主要道路。汉武帝派张骞出使西域后形成其基本干道。它以西汉时期长安为起点（东汉时为洛阳），经河西走廊到敦煌。从敦煌起分为南北两路：南路从敦煌经楼兰、于阗、莎车，穿越葱岭今帕米尔到大月氏、安息，往西到达条支、大秦；北路从敦煌到交河、龟兹、疏勒，穿越葱岭到大宛，往西经安息到达大秦。

历史沿革

丝绸之路通常是指欧亚大陆北部的商路，与南方的茶马古道形成对比，西汉汉武帝时派出张骞从长安带队出使西域，联合大月氏人共同抗击匈奴。首次开拓丝绸之路，被称为“凿空之旅”。此后，汉朝频繁的派出使节出使西方，汉武帝时期最远的汉使到了犁轩（今埃及亚利山大港），罗马人征服叙利亚的塞琉西帝国和埃及的托勒密王朝后，通过安息帝国、贵霜帝国和阿克苏姆帝国取得从丝绸之路上传来的中国丝绸。西汉末年，丝绸之路曾一度断绝，直到东汉被班超重新打通，罗马帝国的使者也首次顺着丝路来到当时东汉首都洛阳。在通过这条漫漫长路进行贸易的货物中，中国的丝绸无疑最具代表性，“丝绸之路”因此得名。丝绸之路不仅是古代亚欧互通有无的商贸大道，还是促进亚欧各国与中国的友好往来的，是沟通东西方文化的友谊之路。历史上一些著名人物，如出使西域的张骞，投笔从戎的班超，西天取经的玄奘等等，他们的传奇故事都与这条路息息相关。

丝路前身

丝绸之路开通以前，中原与欧亚草原之间就存在着密切的文化交流。中原青铜器、车器、兵器等常常出现在中国北方地区草原民族的墓葬中。战国时期中原的丝绸、漆器、铜镜等经由草原民族远播至新疆、哈萨克斯坦阿尔泰地区以及更遥远的希腊，欧亚草原流行的动物纹样由西至东传入中国北方地区，被包括秦国工匠在内的中国工匠借鉴和创新，形成了一种全新的具有浓郁草原风情的神兽纹样。这种神兽纹样受到中原国家的的青睐，被用来装饰马具、漆器、饰贝腰带的腰饰牌等，甚至在西汉早期还形成一种贵族时尚流行于西汉王朝。同时，西方的玻璃制品、金银器等也经由草原地区传入中国。汉代的“丝绸之路”正是在古代的这样一条贸易交流的道路上发展而来的。

凿空西域

西汉时，阳关和玉门关以西（即今新疆乃至更远）的地方被称作西域。西汉初期，联络东西方的通道被匈奴所阻。汉武帝时开始加强对西域的经略。除了派出兵马攻打匈奴之外，他还遣张骞从长安带队出使西域，联合大月氏人，共同抗击匈奴。虽然最终张骞始终未能说服月氏人与汉朝联盟夹击匈奴，但其产生的实际影响和所起的历史作用是巨大的。他第一次通使西域，使中国的影响直达葱岭以西。自此，不仅西域同内地的联系日益加强，而且中国同中亚、西亚，以至南欧的直接交往也建立和密切起来。史学家司马迁称赞张骞出使西域为“凿空”，意思是“开通大道”。元狩四年，汉武帝再任张骞为中郎将，携带金币丝帛等财物数千巨万，牛羊万头，第二次出使西域。虽然张骞到达乌孙时，恰逢乌孙内乱，因此没有达到劝说乌孙东归的目的。不过，张骞的副使分别访问了中亚的大宛、康居、大月氏、大夏等国，这不仅扩大了西汉王朝的政治影响，增强了相互间的文化了解。

此后，汉朝频繁地派出使节出使西方，汉武帝时期汉使最远曾到达到犁轩（今埃及亚利山大港）。张骞两次出使西域，为中国赢得了贸易、建设和统一的保障，促进了东西经济文化交流，对东西方历史都具有深远的意义。此后，汉朝和西域各国经常互派使者进行交流。这促进了双方贸易的发展，形成了商胡贩客，日款于塞下的景象。西域的天马、汗血马等良种马，葡萄、核桃、苜蓿、石榴、胡萝卜和地毯等传入内地，丰富了汉族人民的经济生活。汉族的铸铁、开渠、凿井等技术和丝织品、金属工具等，传到了西域，促进了西域的经济发展。

远播欧洲

西汉末年，西域诸国断绝了与新莽政权的联系，丝绸之路一度中断。直至公元 73 年，东汉班超随从大将军窦固出击北匈奴，并奉命出使西域。他率领吏士 36 人首先来到鄯善，以“不入虎穴，焉得虎子”的决心，使鄯善为之震服。之后他又说服于阗，归附中央政府。班超重新打通隔绝数十年的丝绸之路，并帮助西域各国摆脱了匈奴的控制，被东汉任命为西域都护。班超在西域经营的 30 年期间，加强了西域与内地的联系。公元 97 年，班超派出副使甘英出使大秦国（罗马帝国），一直到达条支海（今波斯湾），这次的行程将丝绸之路从亚洲延伸到了欧洲，再次打通已经衰落的丝绸之路。

公元 100 年，罗马帝国属下的蒙奇兜讷（今译为马其顿）地区遣使来到东汉首都洛阳，向汉和帝进献礼物。汉和帝厚待两国使者，赐给两国国王代表最高荣誉的紫绶金印，表示了邦交上的极大诚意，这也是罗马帝国与中国通使交往的最早记载。 公元 166 年，半个多世纪之后，古罗马大秦王安敦派使者来到洛阳朝见汉桓帝，标志着中西方文化交往的开始，东西方两大帝国外交关系正式建立。

丝路千年

魏晋南北朝时期 丝绸之路不断发展，主要有西北丝绸之路（又叫绿洲丝绸之路或沙漠丝绸之路）、西南丝绸之路（又叫永昌丝绸之路）和海上丝绸之路三条。它具有由两汉到隋唐的过渡性、海上丝绸之路进一步发展、南北两政权同时与西域频繁交往这三方面的特点。

北魏文成帝太安元年（公元 455 年），在交往断绝了很长一段时间后，波斯与统一了中国北方的北魏王朝建立了直接的联系。从这时开始直到公元 522 年，《魏书》本纪记载了十个波斯使团，前五次到达北魏都城平城（今山西大同）为中国带来了玻璃制品工艺，后五次到达公元 493 年迁都后的洛阳的历史事件。《洛阳伽蓝记》记载了当时丝绸之路上来往的商贩的繁盛情况：“自葱岭以西，至于大秦，百国千城，莫不附焉，胡商贩客，日奔塞下”。北魏王朝还在洛阳城南的伊洛之间设四夷馆、四夷里招待丝路客商。同时，波斯的使者也顺着丝绸之路深入到南朝。中大通二年（公元 530 年），波斯国遣使献佛牙。五年（公元 533 年）八月，遣使献方物。

大同元年（公元 535 年）四月又献方物。

这一时期，中西之间的交流主要体现在政治、经济、文化三方面。这种交流，在政治上，促进了东西方之间的联系与交流；在经济上，促进了双方之间经济贸易、生产技术的交流；在文化上，促进了中国佛教的兴盛和礼乐文化的发展。

隋唐时期　隋炀帝即位后，有经略四方之志。他一方面进行军事扩张，开拓疆域；一方面遣使与海、陆两道丝路沿途国家进行交通。大业年间，隋炀帝遣使侍御史韦节、司隶从事杜行满出使西域各国，展开了与西域的联系和交往，从西域获得玛瑙杯、佛经等奇珍异物，韦节回国后撰有《西蕃记》一书。韦节等人的出使，扩大了隋对西域的了解，打破了中原地区与西域的长期隔绝状态。隋朝中期，张掖成为当时的中西贸易中心，西域诸国都在此地与中国互市，兴盛时曾有四十多个西域国家的商人集中在这里经商。为了增进对西域的了解，扩大与西域诸国的贸易活动，在韦节等出使西域不久，炀帝又派遣裴矩前往张掖主持互市。裴矩的工作卓有成效，大业年间，西域“相率来朝者”大约有三十余国。裴矩经过搜寻资料，采访胡人，亲自撰写完成了《西域图记》（三卷），这部书中除了记载西域诸国的山川地理、风俗物产等情况外，最可贵的是记下了通往西域的三条最主要的道路。裴矩将它们称为北道、中道和南道，比之《魏书・西域传》所记的更加具体，代表了隋时对西域各国的认识水平。

裴矩对西域的经营，保证了丝绸之路的畅通，使“西域诸蕃，往来相继”，中原地区与西域各国重新加强了经济贸易方面的往来。炀帝时，西域三十余国频至中原“朝贡”，西域诸国商胡也纷纷来长安、洛阳等地经商。炀帝在大兴（今西安）建国门外设立四方馆，以待四方使客，各掌其方国及互市事。因西域诸国朝贡者多，于是炀帝大业六年时，又征四方奇技异艺之士在洛阳皇城端门外举行盛会，并令洛阳东三市（东市、西市、南市）店铺皆设帷帐，盛列酒食，邀请西域诸蕃酋长、各国使者和胡商参加，集娱乐、贸易为一体。这长达一个月的贸易盛会具有国际性质，显示了隋时中外交流的盛况。

唐代时，丝绸之路发展到了一个新时期。实行“关中本位政策”的唐政府一直致力于西北地区的开发。唐朝初期，西域虽大都处在西突厥控制之下，但西域各国国王都曾派人或亲自到大唐，表示归附，因此唐初很快便恢复了丝路交通。贞观四年（公元 630 年），伊吉城主归附于唐，唐在这里设置伊州，控制了西域北道。这时，在西域地区拥有较强政权的高昌为了垄断丝绸贸易，封闭了西域南部进入中原的道路，商贾都要经过高昌，并需交纳商税。贞观十四年（公元 640 年）唐政府派侯君集带兵平定了高昌，在高昌设西州，置西州刺史，不久后又在这里设置安西都护府，屯驻军队，镇守整个西域地区。在平定高昌的同一年，驻守于可汗浮图域（今吉木萨尔以北）的西突厥叶护归唐，唐政府在这里设庭州，置庭州刺史，唐又将伊州、西州、庭州划入陇右道，加强了对这一地区的管理。

在此过程中，太宗李世民为东西方交流做出的贡献极为巨大，他击败东突厥吐谷浑，臣服漠南北，之后唐高宗又灭西突厥。至武则天女皇时，已设安西、北庭两都护府，安西都护府又辖龟兹、碎叶、于阗、疏勒四镇。唐朝疆域，东起朝鲜海滨，西至达昌水（阿姆河，一说底格里斯河），不久便与新兴的撒拉逊帝国（阿剌伯帝国，大食）接壤。而唐王朝则成为了当时世界第一的发达强盛国家，经济文化发展水平都居世界前列。这样，东西方开始通过丝绸之路，以大食帝国为桥梁，官方、民间都进行了全面友好的交往。

随着唐政府对丝路的开发，尤其是隋唐大运河的投入航运，江南富庶区与中原地区的联系大大增强，南方的丝绸、瓷器、茶叶等商品源源不断的通过大运河运送到洛阳、长安两京并通过丝绸之路远销西方受到这条复兴了的贸易路线巨大影响的国家还有日本。8 世纪，日本遣唐使节带来了很多西域文物到日本首都奈良，这些宝贵古代文物现代也在奈良正仓院保存下来，日本最大的宗教佛教也是通过丝绸之路传来的。唐代丝绸之路的畅通繁荣，进一步促进了东西方思想文化交流，对以后相互的社会和民族意识形态发展，产生了很多积极、深远的影响。

宋元时期　宋元时，相比于陆上丝绸之路，海上丝绸之路更为繁荣发展。在唐朝中期以前，中国对外主通道是陆上丝绸之路，之后由于战乱及经济重心转移等原因，海上丝绸之路逐渐取代陆路成为中外贸易交流主通道，在宋元时期范围覆盖大半个地球，是人类历史活动和东西方文化经济交流的重要载体。海上通道在隋唐时运送的主要大宗货物仍是丝绸，所以后世把这条连接东西方的海道叫作海上丝绸之路。到了宋元时期，瓷器出口渐成为主要货物，因此又称作“海上陶瓷之路”。同时由于输出商品有很大一部分是香料，因此也被称为“海上香料之路”，海上丝绸之路是约定俗成的统称。尤其是在宋元时期，中国造船技术和航海技术的大幅提升以及指南针的航海运用，全面提升了商船远航能力，私人海上贸易也得到发展。这一时期，中国同世界 60 多个国家有着直接的“海上丝路”商贸往来。

蒙元时，成吉思汗为了征服亚欧大陆，除了以武力掠夺邻近外族财富外，还大力借助回回商队的长途贩运来筹措军饷，曾多次派遣一些商队前往中亚务国进行贸易。公元 1218 年，一支由蒙古帝国出资组织的四百五十人的商队，装运大批毛皮、丝绸、金银制品前往中亚花剌子模贸易，但花剌子模却劫夺了这批货物，这次事件成为蒙古大军第一次西征的导火线。在三次西征及南征后，蒙元帝国版图大大扩展。加之驿路的设立、欧亚交通网络的恢复，欧亚广大地域范围内国际商队长途贩运活动再度兴盛起来。蒙元时期中外关系史的一些名著，如《马可・波罗游记》、《通商指南》、《柏朗嘉宾蒙古行记》、《卢布鲁克东行记》、《大可汗国记》、《马黎诺里游记》、《鄂多立克东游录》等都大量记载了丝绸之路上商队贸易的情况。

根据史料记载，当时在漫长的东西方陆路商道上从事商队贩运贸易的，有欧洲拜占庭帝国的君士坦丁堡、波兰、奥地利、捷克、俄国、意大利威尼斯、热那亚以及早期北欧汉撒同盟等地的商人，有由西域蒙古诸汗国及其后裔统治的西亚、中亚地区的商人以及中国色目商人等等。元代来中国的外国商人、商队为数之众，在外国史料中多有印证。《马可・波罗游记》中几处写道：“元大都外城常有‘无数商人’、‘大量商人’来往止息，‘建有许多旅馆和招待骆驼商队的大客栈，……旅客按不同的人种，分别下榻在指定的彼此隔离的旅馆’。”既为不同人种，则无疑为外国客商。《通商指南》也指出，“……汗八里都城商务最盛。各国商贾辐辏于此，百货云集”。欧州和中、西亚商人一般都携带大量金银、珠宝、药物、奇禽异兽、香料、竹布等商品来中国或在沿途出售，他们所购买的主要是中国的缎匹、绣彩、金锦、丝绸、茶叶、瓷器、药材等商品。由于从欧洲到中国路程十分遥远、沿途地理气候条件也非常复杂险恶，所以商人的长途贩运，一般都必须级成数十人以上的商队结伴而行，且需随地雇佣翻译、随带必要的食品、什物、料草等。

在蒙元时期丝路畅通、欧亚大陆各种层次的经济交流兴旺之际，作为东西方国际贸易枢纽，民族性商品市场和物资集散地的一批贸易中心相应形成和发展。当时从西方到东方，有一些较大的贸易中心，如元大都，西方人称为汗八里（今北京）。元代中外史籍几乎都记述了元大都作为东方国际贸易中心的无可争议的地位。这里“各国商贾辐辏，百货云集”。《马可・波罗游记》曾以一章的篇幅介绍元大都国际贸易的盛况：“凡世界上最为珍奇宝贵的东西，都能在这座城市找到，……这里出售的商品数量，比其他任何地方都多”。元朝中国境内丝路重要商镇还有可失哈耳（喀什噶尔），这里的纺织品“由国内的商人运销世界各地”；河西走廊的肃州，这里附近“山上出产的一种质量非常好的大黄。别处的商人都来这里采购，然后行销世界各地”；另外还有别失八里、哈喇火州等地。

路线走向

丝绸之路是历史上横贯欧亚大陆的世界贸易交通主道，其基本走向定于两汉时期。陆上丝路因地理走向不一，又分为“北方丝路”与“南方丝路”；因所经地区的地理景观差异很大，又被它细分为“草原森林丝路”、“高山峡谷丝路”和“沙漠绿洲丝路”。

北方丝路　北方陆上丝路指由黄河中下游通达西域的商路，自玉门关、阳关出西域有两道：从鄯善，傍南山北，波河西行，至莎车为南道，南道西逾葱岭则出大月氏、安息；自车师前王庭（今吐鲁番），随北山，波河西行至疏勒（今喀什）为北道，北道西逾葱岭则出大宛、康居、奄蔡（黑海、咸海间）。北道上有两条重要岔道：一是由焉耆西南行，穿塔克拉玛干沙漠至南道的于阗；一是从龟兹（今库车）西行过姑墨（阿克苏）、温宿（乌什），翻拔达岭（别垒里山口），经赤谷城（乌孙首府），西行至怛罗斯。

由于南北两道穿行在白龙堆、哈拉顺和塔克拉玛干大沙漠，条件恶劣，道路艰难。于是东汉时在北道之北另开一道，隋唐时成为一条重要通道，称新北道。原来的汉北道改称中道。新北道由敦煌西北行，经伊吾（哈密）、蒲类海（今巴里坤湖）、北庭（吉木萨尔）、轮台（半泉）、弓月城（霍城）、碎叶（托克玛克）至怛罗斯。丝路西段涉及范围较广，包括中亚、南亚、西亚和欧洲，历史上的国家众多，民族关系复杂，因而路线常有变化，大体可分为南、中、北 3 道：

①南道由葱岭西行，越兴都库什山至阿富汗喀布尔后分两路，一西行至赫拉特，与经兰氏城而来的中道相会，再西行穿巴格达、大马士革，抵地中海东岸西顿或贝鲁特，由海路转至罗马；另一线从白沙瓦南下抵南亚。

②中道（汉北道）越葱岭至兰氏城西北行，一条与南道会，一条过德黑兰与南道会。

③北新道也分两支，一经钹汗（今费尔干纳）、康（今撒马尔罕）、安（今布哈拉）至木鹿与中道会西行；一经怛罗斯，沿锡尔河西北行，绕过咸海、里海北岸，至亚速海东岸的塔那，由水路转刻赤，抵君士坦丁堡（今伊斯坦布尔）。

南方丝路　南方陆上丝路即“蜀—身毒道”，因穿行于横断山区，又称高山峡谷丝路。大约公元前 4 世纪，中原群雄割据，蜀地（今川西平原）与身毒间开辟了一条丝路，延续两个多世纪尚未被中原人所知，所以有人称它为秘密丝路。直至张骞出使西域，在大夏发现蜀布、邛竹杖是从身毒转贩而来的，由此向汉武帝报告后，于元狩元年（公元前 122 年）打通“蜀—身毒道”。蜀—身毒道从今四川起始，经云南的昭通、曲靖、大理，从保山出境入缅甸、泰国，到达印度，再从印度翻山越海抵达中亚，然后直至地中海沿岸。在这条古商道上，中国商人与掸国（今缅甸）或身毒（即印度）的商人进行货物交换，用丝绸或邛竹杖，换回金、贝、玉石、琥珀、琉璃制品等。

南方丝路由 3 条道组成，即灵关道、五尺道和永昌道。丝路从成都出发分东、西两支，东支沿岷江至僰道（今宜宾），过石门关，经朱提（今昭通）、汉阳（今赫章）、味（今曲靖）、滇（今昆明）至叶榆（今大理），是谓五尺道；西支由成都经临邛（今邛崃）、严关（今雅安）、莋（今汉源）、邛都（今西昌）、盐源、青岭（今大姚）、大勃弄（今祥云）至叶榆，称之灵关道。两线在叶榆会合，西南行过博南（今永平）、巂唐（今保山）、滇越（今腾冲），经掸国（今缅甸）至身毒。

南方陆上丝路延续 2000 多年，特别是在抗日战争期间，由于大后方出海通道被切断，故沿丝路西南道开辟的滇缅公路、中印公路运输空前繁忙，成为支援后方的生命线。

The Silk Road

Eurasia is a magical land, which gave birth to the ancient Chinese civilization, ancient Babylonian civilization, ancient Greek civilization, ancient Egyptian civilization and ancient Indian civilization. Five ancient and excellent civilizations also make the Eurasia play a major role being the core areas in the development of world. The ancient Chinese civilization is the only surviving ancient civilization that has been developing vividly so far.

The Chinese nation has continued ever since, just because Chinese emphasis on the unity of nature and philosophy and follow the principles of harmony in diversity. China is a peace-loving nation, they have the courage to explore the outside world, and always maintain a friendly and tolerant attitude. The emperor sent Zhang Qian to the Western Regions in the Western Han Dynasty. Then they created the commercial channel to connect the Mediterranean countries from Chang’an. In late 19 century, a German geographer Ferdinand von Richthofen called it as “The Silk

Road" in his book for that China is the hometown of silk. After then, historians collectively called the commercial channel between Chinese and western as the Silk Road. The Silk Road spans more than 2000 years and involves land and sea, so it should be divided to four times: the Pre-Qin, Han and Tang Dynasties, Song and Yuan Dynasties, Ming and Qing Dynasties according to history, also divided into Land Silk Road and Marine Silk Road according to the circuit. Before the middle of the Tang Dynasty, China's foreign main channel was Land Silk Road. Due to war and economic shift, Land Silk Road was gradually replaced by "Marine Silk Road" as main foreign trade channel. In fact, the prototype of the Marine Silk Road has existed throughout the period of Qin and Han Dynasties, developed in Wei and Jin Dynasties, flourishing in Sui and Tang Dynasties, reached the peak during Song and Yuan period. Whether Land Silk Road or Marine Silk Road, they both reflect that ancient Chinese people seek to communicate with the outside world actively, desire peace and connection, have the courage to explore and adventure.

"Land Silk Road"

The Silk Road began in ancient China. It is commercial trade route connecting Asia, Africa and Europe, also known as the Stone Road, the Buddhism road, and the Spices Road. "Land Silk Road" formed between the 2nd century B.C. and the 1st century A.D. it was a major road for economic, political and cultural exchanges between the East and the West, which still used in 16th century. It started from Chang' an in Western Han Dynasty to Dunhuang crossing Hexi Corridor. It was divided into two roads from Dunhuang, north and south. South road started from Dunhuang Loulan, Khotan, Yarkand, through green ridge Pamir to DaRouzhi, Parthia. North road started from Dunhuang to Jiaohe, Qiuci, Shule, through the green ridge to Dayuan, toward the west arrived in Daqin.

History

The Silk Road usually refers to the trade routes of northern Eurasian, contrasting to Tea Horse Road in the south. Emperor Wu of Han has sent envoys to the west frequently since Zhang Qian explored the Silk Road. The envoy ever reached Alexandria in the period of Emperor Wu. The Romans got Chinese silk from the Silk Road through Parthian Empire, Kushan Empire and Kingdom of Aksum. At the end of the West Han Dynasty, the Silk Road had been cut off. Ban Chao got it through until the East Han Dynasty. The Roman envoy came to Luoyang along the Silk Road for the first time in the East Han Dynasty. Silk is the most representative among trade goods through the Road, so it is named as "The Silk Road". The Silk Road is not only an exchange channel in the ancient Eurasian, but also a road of friendship between eastern and western culture, promoting Asia-Europe countries to communicate with China. Some famous person in history, such as Zhang Qian, Ban Chao, Xuanzang etc., are closely related to the Silk Road.

The predecessor of the Silk Road

Before the opening of the Silk Road, there existed a close culture exchange between the central plains and the Eurasian. For instance, Ancient bronze weapons and equips often appeared in the tombs of north grasslands. Glass and treasure of west countries was also introduced into China through the prairie region. The Silk Road of Han Dynasty just developed from an ancient trade exchanges channel.

Explored the way from the Central China to the West

In the West Han Dynasty, the Western Regions refers to west of Yang Pass and Yumen Pass. In the Early West Han Dynasty, the Huns blocked the channel that linked the east and the west. Emperor Wu began to strengthen the management of the Western Regions. Besides sent troops beat against the Huns, he ordered Zhang Qian to lead one hundred people to adventure the west, and combine the Rouzhi to defeat the Huns. Although Zhang Qian failed to persuade the Rouzhi to make alliance with Han Dynasty, he has made great influence in the history. Zhang Qian ' s travel to the western regions made the influence of China cross Congling Mountains. From then on, the connection between the western regions and the mainland was strengthening day by day. And the Han Dynasty began to build up friendly relationship with Central Asia, West Asia, and even south Europe. In 121B.C, the Emperor sent Zhang Qian to make alliance with Wusun with identity of Zhonglangjiang. They took millions of cattle, sheep, silk and gold to the western regions. When he arrived in Wusun Kingdom, civil strife broke out there. So he did not complete the mission. Zhang Qian sent his assistants to the countries for diplomatic activities such as Dawan, Kangju, the Big Rouzhi and Daxia. The travel not only expanded the political influence of the West Han Dynasty, but also strengthened the mutual cultural understanding.

Since then, the Han Dynasty sent diplomatic to the west frequently. Zhang Qian' s two travels to the western regions won the safeguard for China to trade construction and the unified, promoted the economic, cultural exchanges between China and the West.

Spread to Europe

In late West Han Dynasty, the western regions quit contacting XinMang regimes; the Silk Road was also cut off. Until 73A.C, Ban Chao got the order to beat North Xiongnu and visit the western regions. He leaded thirty-six people to Shanshan (a country in Xingjiang) with firm determination. He persuaded Kingdom of Khotan to join the central government. Ban Chao re-open the Silk Road, which has isolated for decades, and help the western regions get rid of the control of the Huns. He strengthened the relationship between the western regions and the mainland. In 97A.C, Ban Chao sent his assistant, Gan Ying, to Da Qin. This travel made the Silk Road extend from Asia to Europe, revitalize the Silk Road.

In 100A.C, the messengers of Mongolia came to Luoyang, the capital of the East Han Dynasty, and present gifts to the Emperor He. Emperor He favored the messengers and gave purple ribbon gold seal to the Kings, which expressed great sincerity on diplomatic relations. It is also earliest record about the communication between the Rome Empire and China. In 166A.C, more than half century later, the King of Da Qin, An Dun, sent messengers to Luoyang. It marks the beginning of the cultural exchanges between China and the west, and the diplomatic relations of China and the west formally established.

The Millennium Silk Road

Wei Jin and the Northern and Southern Dynasties

In the development of the Silk Road, there are three roads in the period: The Northwest Silk Road, the Southwest Silk Road and Marine Silk Road. The characters of the Silk Road are transitional, further development of Marine Silk Road and frequent communication with the western regimes.

In 455, The Persian and the Northern Wei Dynasty established a direct relation after a long-time isolation. "Weishu" (History of Wei) recorded, ten Persian missions have come to China ten times from 445 to 522. They brought the technology of glass products to Chinese. " Temples and Monasteries in Luoyang" ever recorded the prosperity of the traders on the Silk Road. The Northern Wei Dynasty set up Siyiguan in the south of Luoyang to receive the foreign businessman from the Silk Road. Meanwhile, The Persian messengers went to the Southern Dynasties along the Silk Road. In 530， The Persian offered the Tooth Relic. In 533 and 535, The Persian presented gifts to China.

During this period, communication between China and the west was mainly manifested in three aspects: politics, economy, culture. In politics, it promoted the communication between east and west, in economy, it promoted the communication of economic, trade, production technology between both sides, in culture, it promoted the rise of the Chinese Buddhism and the development of rites and music culture.

Sui and Tang Dynasty

After Emperor Yang of Sui, one hand, he sought military expansion and made a new frontier, on the other hand, he sent missions to communicate with the countries along the Silk Road. In 600s, Emperor Yang sent Wei Jie to the western regimes, and got lots of foreign treasures, such as agateware, Buddhist sutras. Wei Jie wrote "Xifanji" to record the experience. In the middle of Sui Dynasty, Zhangye became the center of foreign trade. There have been numbers of businessmen from more than forty countries trading here. To enhance the understanding of the Western Regions and expand trade activities, Pei Ju was sent to preside business activities in Zhangye. Very good results have been achieved during his term of office. Pei Ju ever wrote "Picture of the Western Regions" . Except for geography, customs and products, the book recorded three main roads to the Western Regimes. Pei named them as North Road, Middle Road and South Road. Compared with "Weishu" , it was much more detailed, which represented the level of understanding of the western countries.

Pei Ju ensured the smooth flow of the Silk Road. The economic and trade exchanges between the Central Plains and the western countries were strengthened again. In the era of Emperor Yang, more than thirty countries from the Western Regimes came to China to pay tribute. And businessmen came to Chang' an for trading. So "Sifangguan" was set up to serve envoys. In 610, Emperor Yang held the event to entertain guests from the Western Regimes. The one-month event was an international activity, which shows the grand occasion between China and the west in Sui Dynasty.

In Tang Dynasty, The Silk Road has developed into a new era. The government has been committed to the development of the northwest region. In the early Tang Dynasty, although most areas of the Western Regimes were under the control of Western Turkic Khaganate, all of Kings have come to Chang' an to join Tang Dynasty. So the Silk Road was recover soon. In 630, Yizhou was set, which control the North Road. Later, Gaochang (a strong power in the Western Regimes) closed South Road to the Central Plains. The businessmen need to pay tax when pass Gaochang. In 640, the Tang government sent Hou Junji to lead troops to suppress Gaochang and strengthen the management of the region.

The emperor Li Shimin made great contributions to the communication between Eastern and western. In the era of Emperor Wu, Tang Dynasty has become the most developed country of the world. Since then, official and folk communicate in more comprehensive and friendly way along the Silk Road.

With the development of the Silk Road, especially great input of the Grand Canal in the Sui and Tang Dynasties, the relation between Jiangnan and the Central Plains is enhanced. Silk, porcelain and tea reached Luoyang, Chang' an and even the West. The Silk Road also has huge impact on Japan. In 8th century, messengers carried lots of Western cultural relics to the capital of Japan, which still kept in the Shosoin of Nara. The prosperity of the Silk Road in the Tang Dynasty has further promoted the ideological and cultural exchanges between the East and the West. It has produced a lot of positive and far-reaching influence on the development of mutual social and national ideology.

Song and Yuan Dynasty

In Song and Yuan Dynasty, compared with land Silk Road, Marine Silk Road was much more prospective. Before middle of the Tang Dynasty, land Silk Road was main trade channel. Due to war and economic shift, Land Silk Road was gradually replaced by "Marine Silk Road" as main foreign trade channel. It has covered half the world in Song and Yuan. Main commodity was silk in Sui and Tang, so it was called Marine Silk Road. In Song and Yuan, China gradually became the main export goods. So it was called "the Porcelain Road" . Meantime, Spices were also a big part, and then it was called "the Spices Road" . They were collectively called Marine Silk Road. As the development of Shipbuilding technology and navigation technology and the use of the compass, merchant sailing had great advanced. At that period, China had a direct "maritime Silk Road" business with more than 60 countries in the world.

To conquer Asia and Europe, Genghis Khan robbed wealth from the neighborhood and sent travelling merchants to countries in Central Asia for financing of wars. In 1218, a caravan of 450 men went to Khwarezm with a large number of furs, silk, gold and silver products. But the Khwarezm robbed the goods. This event became the fuse of Mongolia' s first expedition. The Yuan Empire expanded greatly after three expeditions. International long-distance business activities flourished again in Asia and Europe. Some famous works on the history of Chinese and foreign relations in Yuan Dynasty, The Travels of Marco Polo, Trade Guide，Mongolia trip，have recorded the trading activities on the Silk Road.

According to historical records，the businessmen from Constantinople, Poland, Austria, Czech, Russia, Italy, Genoa, the early Nordic Hanseatic League, the western Mongolia Khanate and Semu people were ever engaged in the trade activities on the Silk Road. Many foreign historical data confirmed it. The Travels of Marco Polo wrote: "there were numbers of businessmen around the capital of Yuan……Many hotels were built for the caravan……Passengers were staying at designated hotels according to different ethnic groups." Trade Guide pointed: "Commodity and merchants from all over the world gathered here……" Generally, they carried large amounts of gold and silver jewelry, drugs, rare animals, spices, bamboo and other goods to China or along the way to sell. What they buy is mainly Chinese satin, embroidered color, gold brocade, silk, tea, porcelain, medicinal herbs and other products. Due to the complicated geography and climate, the caravan usually consisted of more than ten persons, including translations, with the necessary food, sundries and feed grass.

In Yuan Dynasty, economic communications in Asia and Europe at various levels were flourishing. As the international trades hub of the East and the West, a number of national commodity markets and trade centers came into being and developed. Chinese and foreign history almost all described the capital of Yuan as Oriental International Trade Center, which had undisputed status. The Travels of Marco Polo ever wrote: "the most precious goods can be found in the city……The number of goods sold here is more than anywhere else."

Routes

The Silk Road was a main trade channel across Asia and Europe in the history. In the Han dynasty, the Silk Road was divided into "the North Silk Road" and "the South Silk Road". Because the geographical landscape of the region is very different, it is subdivided into "forest and grassland Silk Road", "high mountain valley Silk Road" and "desert oasis Silk Road".

The North Silk Road

The North Silk Road was a trade route from Middle and Lower Yellow River to the Western Regimes. There were two directions; South Road was from Shanshan, along the north of South Mountain, to Shache. North Road was from Turpan, along North Mountain and Po rivers, to Kashgar. There were two important branch roads on North Road. One started from Yanqi, through the Taklimakan Desert, to khotan, the other started from Qiuci, through Gumo (Aksu), Wensu (Wushi), passed the Red Valley (capital of the Wusun), to Mazda Ross.

Because two roads went through the white dragon heap, Sahara and the Taklimakan Desert, the conditions were tough. Another road stared to the north of North Road and become an important channel in Sui Dynasty, called as new North Road. The old one was called as Middle Road. New North Road started from Dunhuang, passed Hami, Barkol Lake, Jimsar, Banquan and Gong Yue city to Mazda. The western part of the Silk Road involved a wide range, including Central Asia, South Asia, West Asia and Europe. It was divided into three road: south, middle and north.

The South Silk Road

The South Silk Road went through Hengduan Mountain, so it was called as high mountain valley Silk Road. In 4th century B.C, the Central Plains was separated. The road was unknown by people until Zhang Qian went to the Western Regions, it was also called as secret Silk Road. In 122 B.C, the road was got through. It started Yunnan, passed Burma, Thailand, reached India and even Mediterranean coast. Chinese businessmen bartering silk for shellfish, jade, amber and glass products with Burmese and Indian.

The Southern Silk Road consisted of three roads, namely Lingguan Road, Wuchi Road and Yongchang Road. The South Silk Road lasted 2000 years. Especially in the period of the war of resistance against Japan, the rear road to the sea was cut off, so the Burma Road and China India highway along the Southwest Silk Road were busy. They became lifelines for supporting.

海上丝绸之路

Maritime Silk Road

海上丝绸之路

“海上丝绸之路”是古代中国与外国交通贸易和文化交往的海上通道，该路主要以南海为中心，所以又称“南海丝绸之路”。古代海上丝绸之路从中国东南沿海，经过中南半岛和南海诸国，穿过印度洋，进入红海，抵达东非和欧洲，成为中国与外国贸易往来和文化交流的海上大通道，并推动了沿线各国的共同发展。海上丝绸之路形成于秦汉时期，发展于三国至隋朝时期，繁荣于唐宋时期，转变于明清时期，是已知的最为古老的海上航线。

历史沿革

秦代　海上丝绸之路的雏形早已存在，目前已知有关中外海路交流的最早史载来自《汉书·地理志》，当时中国就与南海诸国接触，而有遗迹实物出土表明中外交流可能更早于汉代。而中国丝绸的输出，早在公元前，便已有东海与南海两条起航线。

两汉　西汉中晚期和东汉时期海上丝绸之路真正形成并开始发展。西汉时期，南方南粤国与印度半岛之间的海路已经开通。汉武帝灭南越国后，凭借海路拓宽了海贸规模，这时“海上丝绸之路”兴起。东汉时期还记载了与罗马帝国的第一次来往：中国商人由海路到达广州进行贸易，运送丝绸、瓷器经海路由马六甲经苏门答腊来到印度，并采购香料、染料运回中国；印度商人再把丝绸、瓷器经过红海运往埃及的开罗港，或经波斯湾进入两河流域到达安条克，再由希腊、罗马商人从埃及的亚历山大、加沙等港口经地中海运往希腊、罗马两大帝国的大小城邦。这标志着横贯亚、非、欧三大洲的、真正意义的海上丝绸之路的形成，从中国广东番禺、徐闻、广西合浦等港口启航西行，与从地中海、波斯湾、印度洋沿海港口出发往东航行的海上航线，在印度洋上相遇并实现了对接，广东成为海上丝绸之路的始发地。随着汉代种桑养蚕和纺织业的发展，丝织品成为这一时期的主要输出品。

三国　汉末三国处于丝绸之路从陆地转向海洋的承前启后与海上丝绸之路最终形成的关键时期。由于同曹魏、刘蜀在长江上作战与海上交通的需要，孙吴积极发展水军，船舰的设计与制造有了很大进步，技术先进，规模也很大。三国之后的其他南方政权（东晋、宋、齐、梁、陈）也一直与北方对峙，也推动了造船、航海技术的发展，航海经验的积累为海上丝绸之路发展提供了良好条件。

魏晋　魏晋以后，海上丝绸之路形成：以广州为起点，经海南岛东面海域，直穿西沙群岛海面抵达南海诸国，再穿过马六甲海峡，直驶印度洋、红海、波斯湾，对外贸易涉及 15 个国家和地区，此时丝绸是主要的输出品。

隋唐　在隋唐以前，即公元6世纪至7世纪，海上丝绸之路只是陆上丝绸之路的一种补充形式。但到了隋唐时期，由于西域战火不断，陆上丝绸之路被战争阻断，代之而兴的便是海上丝绸之路。伴随着我国造船、航海技术的发展，通往东南亚、马六甲海峡、印度洋、红海，以及非洲大陆的航路纷纷开通并延伸，海上丝绸之路最终替代陆上丝绸之路，成为我国对外交往的主要通道。根据《新唐书·地理志》记载，唐时，我国东南沿海有一条通往东南亚、印度洋北部诸国、红海沿岸、东北非和波斯湾诸国的海上航路，叫作“广州通海夷道”，这便是我国海上丝绸之路的最早叫法。当时通过这条通道往外输出的商品主要有丝绸、瓷器、茶叶和铜铁器这四大宗；往回输入的主要是香料、花草等一些供宫廷赏玩的奇珍异宝。

宋代　宋代造船技术和航海技术明显提高，指南针广泛应用于航海，中国商船的远航能力大为加强。宋朝与东南沿海国家绝大多数时间保持着友好关系，广州成为海外贸易第一大港。“元丰市舶条”标志着中国古代外贸管理制度又一个发展阶段的开始，私人海上贸易在政府鼓励下得到极大发展。但是为防止钱币外流，南宋政府于公元 1219 年下令以丝绸、瓷器交换外国的舶来品。这样，中国丝绸和瓷器向外传播的数量日益增多，范围更加扩大。宋代海上丝绸之路的持续发展，大大增加了朝廷和港市的财政深收入，一定程度上促进了经济发展和城市化生活，也为中外文化交流提供了便利条件。

元代　元朝在经济上采用重商主义政策，鼓励海外贸易，同中国贸易的国家和地区已扩大到亚、非、欧、美各大洲，并制定了堪称中国历史上第一部系统性较强的外贸管理法则。海上丝绸之路发展也进入鼎盛时期。宋末至元代时，泉州成为中国第一大港，并与埃及的亚历山大港并称为“世界第一大港”。

明代　明代时，海上丝绸之路航线已扩展至全球，进入极盛时期。向西航行的郑和七下西洋，便是明朝政府组织的大规模航海活动。郑和曾到达亚洲、非洲 39 个国家和地区，对后来达・伽马开辟欧洲到印度的地方航线，以及对麦哲伦的环球航行都具有先导作用。向东航行的“广州—拉丁美洲航线”（1575 年），由广州起航，经澳门出海，至菲律宾马尼拉港，穿过海峡进入太平洋，东行至墨西哥西海岸。

清代　由于明清两代政府实行海禁政策，广州成为中国唯一对外开放的贸易大港。广州的海上丝绸之路贸易比唐、宋两代获得更大的发展，形成了空前的全球性大循环贸易，并一直延续至鸦片战争前夕而不衰。鸦片战争后，中国海权丧失，沿海口岸被迫开放，成为西方倾销商品的市场。从此，海上丝路一蹶不振，进入了衰落期。这种状况贯穿整个民国时期，直至新中国成立前夕。

路线走向及贸易对象

主要港口　海上丝路起于秦汉，兴于隋唐，盛于宋元，明初达到顶峰，明中叶因海禁而衰落。海上丝路的重要起点有泉州、番禺（今广州）、明州（今宁波）、扬州、登州（今蓬莱）、刘家港等，同一朝代的海上丝路起点可能有两处乃至更多。规模最大的港口是广州和泉州。广州从秦汉直到唐宋一直是中国最大的商港。明清实行海禁，广州又成为中国唯一对外开放的港口。泉州发端于唐，宋元时成为东方第一大港。广州、泉州在唐、宋、元时，侨居的外商多达万人，乃至十万人以上。

海上路线　历代海上丝路，亦可分三大航线：

①东洋航线由中国沿海港至朝鲜、日本。

②南洋航线由中国沿海港至东南亚诸国。

③西洋航线由中国沿海港至南亚、阿拉伯和东非沿海诸国。

贸易对象　海上丝绸之路的贸易对象主要有：朝鲜、日本、琉球、位于今中南半岛上的国家、东南亚沿岸岛屿、南亚、伊斯兰世界和欧洲各地（因为此海上丝路多只到阿拉伯，因此其他到欧陆的物品一般由经由阿拉伯人转运）。出口货物主要以丝绸、茶、瓷器、金、银、书籍等等为主，进口货物包括：琉璃、猫眼石、明珠、象牙、香料、金银、宝石、水晶、玛瑙、琥珀、骆驼皮、乳香、没药、安息香、沉香、檀香、卢荟、胡椒、温纳齐等。其中传入中国的国外货物多数经陆上丝路传播。

丝路意义

丝绸之路的开辟是人类文明史上的一个伟大创举，它是古代东西方最长的国际交通路线，是丝路沿线多民族的共同创造，所以又被称为友谊之路。丝绸之路在中西交流上起到了重要的作用，为中国与世界各国的商品交流、

文化交流、宗教交流作出了重大贡献。

商品交流

在丝绸之路上，丝绸与同样原产中国的瓷器成为当时一个东亚强盛文明的象征。各国元首及贵族曾一度以穿着用腓尼基红染过的中国丝绸，家中使用瓷器为富有荣耀的象征。此外，阿富汗的青金石也随着商队的行进不断流入欧亚各地。这种远早于丝绸的贸易品在欧亚大陆的广泛传播为带动欧亚贸易交流做出了贡献，曾是两河流域各国财富的象征。当青金石流传到印度后，被那里的佛教徒供奉为佛教七宝之一，令青金石增添了悠远的宗教色彩。

而葡萄、核桃、胡萝卜、胡椒、胡豆、波菜（又称为波斯菜）、黄瓜（汉时称胡瓜）、石榴等的传播为东亚人的日常饮食增添了更多的选择。西域特产的葡萄酒经过历史的发展融入到中国的传统酒文化当中。商队则从中国主要运出铁器、金器、银器、镜子和其他豪华制品。

东西方相互传入和移植的东西很多，医术、舞蹈、武学和一些著名动植物，都使双方增加了不少视野。汉代习将西方输入的东西冠以胡字，如胡琴、胡瓜、胡萝卜等；唐代则习将它们的名称冠以海字，如海棠、海石榴、海珠（波斯湾珍珠）等。据《唐会典》载，唐王朝曾与三百多个国家和地区相互通使交往，每年取道丝绸之路前来长安这个世界最大都市的各国客人，数目皆以万计，定居中国的，单广州便以千计。

文化交流

21 世纪初已知最古老的印刷品——唐代的《金刚经》就发现于敦煌。造纸术曾经为中国古代科技领先于世界作出了巨大的贡献，然而这种技术似乎只有东亚及南亚部分国家才有发达的造纸工业。随着丝绸之路的开辟，纸制品开始在西域以及更远的地方出现，人们已在在楼兰遗迹的考古发现了 2 世纪的古纸。中亚地区虽然也是用纸，却没有发现造纸工业的证据。很多人认为造纸术的西传为欧洲及中亚带来了一次巨大的变革，而最初这场变革却是残酷的：唐朝与新兴的阿巴斯王朝在中亚的势力摩擦不断。在对中亚政治格局具有强大影响力的怛罗斯战役中，阿拉伯人将中国战俘沿着丝绸之路带回撒马尔罕，而这些战俘中就有长于造纸术的中国工匠。造纸术就这样传播到了世界各地。

西域地区沙漠密布，各国的繁荣与水往往是脱不开关系的。天山与昆仑山脉溶化的雪水是西域的主要补给水源之一。然而收集这些雪水并不是容易的事情，溶化后积聚在山脚的水很短时间就会被蒸发或渗入地下。汉朝派遣的军队囤积在西域发展农业时，流传于山区的坎儿井和井渠技术被同样需要水源的军人使用，并逐步流传至更远的国家。早先西域地区的坎儿井技术究竟是由中国还是波斯传入西域的一直是个有争议的问题。不过井渠技术和穿井法被证实是从中国传向西方的：《史记》中记载，贰师将军李广利率兵攻打大宛，利用断绝水源的方式围困城市。然“宛城中新得汉人知穿井”，令大宛人坚持了很长时间。

中国古代印刷术也是沿丝路逐渐西传的技术之一。在敦煌、吐鲁番等地，已经发现了用于雕版印刷的木刻板和部分纸制品，其中唐代的《金刚经》雕版残本如今仍保存于英国。这说明印刷术在唐代至少已传播至中亚。13 世纪时期，不少欧洲旅行者沿丝绸之路来到中国，并将这种技术带回欧洲。15 世纪时，欧洲人谷腾堡利用印刷术印出了一部《圣经》。1466 年，第一个印刷厂在意大利出现，令这种便于文化传播的技术很快传遍了整个欧洲。

宗教交流

佛教自两汉间传入中国后，至南北朝开始大行于中国，并使之中国化成为了禅宗佛教。佛教文化为中国传统哲学和宋明理学的发展注入了新的血液。佛教的韵律更给中国古诗歌带来了四声平仄的提高，增加音乐节奏的美。它的内容更丰富了中国语言的词汇，像“大千世界”、“不二法门”、“恒河沙数”、“极乐世界”、“放下屠刀，立地成佛”这样数以百计的成语，都成了各阶层的流行语。唐代杜牧有诗曰：“南朝四百八十寺，多少楼台风雨中”，今日尚存的就有北魏嵩山嵩岳塔，唐代长安大雁塔，扶风法门寺，五台山南禅寺，佛光寺，辽代应县木塔，杭州六和塔等等，它们的石砌与木质斗拱建筑，精妙绝伦，鬼斧神工，堪称国宝，国际友人无不叹为观止。这些建筑，大大吸收了印度和西方（印度吸收西方）的建筑技术。唐太宗时，高僧玄奘（公元602年—664年）由陆路经中亚往印度取经、讲学，历时十六年，其所著《大唐西域记》一书，记载了当时印度各国的政治、社会、风土人情，至今仍是印度学者研究印度中世纪历史的头等重要资料。他取回佛教经典657部，唐高宗特在长安建大雁塔使其藏经、译经。其后，高僧义净（公元602年—664年）又由海道去印度，历时十六年，取回佛经400部，所著《南海寄归内法传》、《大唐西域求法高僧传》，向中国介绍了当时南亚各国的文化和生活情况。

景教（亦是天主教派的东正教）在唐初也由东罗马帝国传入了我国。西安碑林的《大秦景教流行中国碑》便是活的见证。尽管它后来并未像佛教、伊斯兰教那样产生过影响，但在东西交往史上，却是一件极有历史意义的大事。唐中期自波斯传入的摩尼教（亦称袄教、拜火教），中国化后被称为“明教”，它相信光明必定战胜黑暗，正义必定铲除邪恶，因此深为不少劳动人民所信奉。唐宋后多次农民起义的领袖，都利用它的教义来组织贫苦农民与封建统治者作战斗，公元1368年建立的明王朝，其建国者便是个明教徒。盛唐时期传入中国的伊斯兰教，也是以中近东大食帝国统治区胡商们作为主要媒介的。它受到唐朝官方的尊重，广州、长安等地开始出现了不少清真寺。中国的造纸术，在盛唐时也传入了大食帝国，不久后便经由它传入了欧洲各国。

成功申遗

2014年6月22日，在卡塔尔多哈举行的第38届世界遗产大会宣布，由中国、哈萨克斯坦、吉尔吉斯斯坦三国联合申报的古丝绸之路的东段——“丝绸之路：长安—天山廊道的路网”成功申报世界文化遗产，成为首例跨国合作、成功申遗的项目。丝绸之路项目被列入《世界遗产名录》，成为中国第32项和第33项世界文化遗产。

新的展望

从西汉张骞首次西域探索之行到丝绸之路的蓬勃发展，中国人从来都是怀揣幸福梦想、满怀热情地把自己创造的物质文明和精神文明的伟大成果分享给世界人民、沿着丝绸之路将它们传向世界各地。中国的丝绸、茶叶、瓷器生产技术和四大发明的伟大成果以及诸子百家的经典学说理论思想，这些中华民族的文明成果通过丝绸之路得以广泛传播和推广，为推进世界文明的延续与发展做出了非常卓越的伟大贡献。与此同时，西域各国的风俗特产、文化习惯、宗教信仰也随着丝绸之路不断传入中国，东西双方在互相交流和学习中共同进步，和平相处。

作为古代东西文明交汇的桥梁，丝绸之路推动了欧亚大陆不同国家和民族之间的相互交流和文化沟通，作为连接中国与世界其他地区的交通路线，丝绸之路不仅是一条商贸物资流通的通道，也是东西方人文、宗教、科技交流的桥梁和纽带。丝绸之路上下三千年，陆海五道连接着亚欧非三大洲，东到东北亚，南至东南亚、南亚，向西贯通中亚、西亚、东欧，远达西欧、东北非海岸，沟通了古巴比伦、古埃及、古印度和古中国这四大文明古国及儒家、伊斯兰教和基督教三大文化圈，促进了中古时期人类社会农耕、游牧及渔猎、商贸、海洋等主要经济形态的相互交往与融合，是人类社会全球化历程中一个重要的阶段。它促进着人类命运共同体的形成，对人类社会的交际与发展做出了巨大贡献。

今天，我们一如既往地踏着祖先的西行足迹，在中华民族再次崛起的同时，把我们物质文明的发展成果和历史文明的精神财富，与世界各国爱好和平的各族人民来共同分享。这是一种文明的延续，也是一个国家和民族的精神血脉的延续，它既要求我们薪火相传、代代守护，更需要我们与时俱进、勇于创新和不懈追求。

传统认为郑和下西洋是世界航海史上的空前壮举，因而郑和被认为是我国古代最早下西洋的外交使节。但是，根据最新披露的考古发现，最早下西洋的外交使节当是唐代中叶的杨良瑶。泾阳县境内的《唐故杨府君神道之碑》记载，杨良瑶（736—806），字良瑶，系云阳县龙云里（今属泾阳县云阳镇）人。杨良瑶系宦官出身，大约生活于唐朝代、德、顺、宪宗时期。

少时以节义为志行，长大后以忠勇为己任。杨在唐肃宗至德年中，也就是西元 756~758 的时候进入了皇帝的宫廷，以一名宦官的身份开始了其充满传奇性的一生奋斗。贞元元年 (785) 四月，受命出使黑衣大食（西亚一带），成为我国第一位航海抵地中海沿岸的外交使节。回国后受命主持修葺历代唐陵，参与洛阳平叛。自从杨良瑶率领外交使团航海出使黑衣大食，其时距今已将近 1230 周年了。这一时间，较之永乐三年（1504）明成祖派遣太监郑和七次率船队远航印度洋西岸，整整早了 620 年。现在，我们既要为郑和下西洋给予世界航海事业的伟大贡献而骄傲，更要为杨良瑶早在公元 8 世纪后期就远航中东的历史壮举而自豪。

Marine Silk Road

Marine Silk Road was a sea channel between Ancient China and foreign countries for trade and cultural exchanges. Its center was South China Sea, so it is also known as “the South China Sea Silk road” . The ancient Marine Silk Road started from the southeast coast of China, across the Indian Ocean, into the Red Sea, arrived in East Africa and Europe, which became sea route for Chinese and foreign trade and cultural exchanges, and promoted the common development of the countries along the road. Marine Silk Road came into being in Qin and Han Dynasties, developed in Wei and Jin Dynasties, flourishing in Tang and Song Dynasties, transformed in Ming and Qing Dynasties. It is known as the oldest sea route.

History

Qin Dynasty

The prototype of the Marine Silk Road has existed. The earliest records about Chinese and foreign exchange was found in Hanshu. At that time Chinese and the South China Sea have contacted, and the relics showed that foreign exchange might be earlier than Han Dynasty. And there have been two sea routes for exporting silk before century.

Han Dynasty

Marine Silk Road formed and began to develop in the middle and late West Han Dynasty and the East Han Dynasty. In the West Han Dynasty, the sea channel between the South and the India Peninsula has been opened. After defeat Yue, Emperor Wu broadened the sea trade scale, then the “maritime Silk Road” raised. In the East Han Dynasty, Chinese businessmen arrived in Guangzhou by sea, carrying silk, porcelain to India, and got spices, dyes back to China. Indian businessmen carried silk and porcelain to the Egypt through the Red Sea, or through Persian Gulf into Mesopotamia then arrived in Antioch, and then Greek and Roman merchants took goods from Alexandria, Egypt to the states of Greece and the Roman Empire. It marks the formation of the Marine Silk Road in true meaning, which traversing Asia, Africa, Europe three continents. Guangdong became the starting point of the Marine Silk Road. With the development of the sericulture and silk textile industry, silk fabrics have become a major export during this period.

The Three Kingdoms

In the Three Kingdoms, the Silk Road transformed from land to sea. It was the key period for the final formation of Marine Silk Road. For the need of combat on Changjiang River, Sun developed the Navy, made great progress on designing and producing ships, with advanced technology and large scale. Later, Other southern regimes (Eastern Jin, song, Qi, Liang and Chen) and the north regimes have been in a stalemate, which promoted the development of shipbuilding and navigation technology. The accumulation of marine experience provides a good condition for the development of the Marine Silk Road.

Wei and Jin Dynasties

Marine Silk Road formed in Wei and Jin Dynasties. It started from Guangzhou, passed east of Hainan Island, straight through Xisha islands, arrived in the countries around the South China Sea, then passed through the Malacca Strait, into the Indian Ocean, red sea, Persian Gulf, involving 15 countries and regions for foreign trades. Silk was the major export during this period.

Sui and Tang Dynasties

In 6th, 7th century, Marine Silk Road was just a supplementary form of Land Silk Road. In Sui and Tang Dynasties, Land Silk Road was blocked by war, and Marine Silk Road replaced. With the development of shipbuilding and navigation technology, the routes to Southeast Asia, the Malacca Strait, India Ocean, the Red Sea, and the African continent were opened and extended. Maritime Silk Road finally became the main channel for foreign exchanges. According to the New History of the Tang Dynasty, there was a route along the southeast coast to Southeast Asia, North Asia, India Ocean, the Red Sea, North Africa and the Persian Gulf countries, called as "Guangzhou Maritime Silk Road". The main export goods were silk, porcelain, tea, bronze and iron. The main import goods were spices, flowers and plants.

Song Dynasty

The technology of Shipbuilding and navigation has significantly improved in Song Dynasty. The compass is widely used in navigation. Guangzhou became the first port of overseas trade. "Laws of Yuanfengshi" marked a new start of the foreign trade management system in ancient China; private marine trade has greatly developed under the encouragement of the government. In 1219, to prevent money outflowing, the government ordered to exchange foreign goods with silk and porcelain. Since then, Chinese silk and porcelain were widely spread, which greatly increased the fiscal revenue, promoted economic development and urbanization, and also provided a convenient condition for cultural exchanges between China and foreign countries.

海上丝绸之路第一人 The first man to take the Silk Road on the sea

海上丝路第一人
大唐使臣
杨良瑶

Yuan Dynasty

The Yuan Dynasty adopted mercantilist policies on the economy to encourage overseas trade. Marine Silk Road also entered its heyday. Quanzhou became the first port in China, and known as "the world' s first port" with Alexandria.

Ming Dynasty

In Ming Dynasty, the Marine Silk Road route has been extended to the world, into the golden age. Zheng He' s seven voyages is a large-scale marine activities organized by the government of the Ming Dynasty. He has arrived 39 countries and regions in Asia and Africa. He has a leading role for Da Gama and Magellan. In 1517, his fleet started from Guangzhou, passed Macao, to Manila Port, across the strait into the Pacific Ocean, east to the west coast of Mexico.

Qing Dynasty

Since the Ming and Qing Dynasties government carried out seafaring prohibition policy, Guangzhou became the only opening trading port. an unprecedented global trade in large circulation was formed in Guangzhou in Qing Dynasty. After the Opium War, China lost the sea power. The coastal port is forced to open and become the market of Western dumping goods. From then on, Marine Silk Road began to decline. The situation was lasted to the eve of new China.

Route and trade object

Main port

Marine Silk Road formed in Qin and Han Dynasties, developed in Sui and Tang Dynasties, flourishing in Song and Yuan Dynasties, reached the peak in early Ming Dynasty, and declined in middle Ming Dynasty. The start ports of Marine Silk Road are Quanzhou, Guangzhou, Ningbo, Yangzhou, Penglai, Liujiagang and so on. The largest ports are Guangzhou and Quanzhou. There were more than one hundred thousand foreign businessmen in Guangzhou, Quanzhou in Tang, Song, and Yuan Dynasties.

Routes

Marine Silk Road can be divided into three major routes:

① east route: from China to Korea and Japan;

② south route: from China to Southeast Asian countries;

③ west route: from China to South Asia, Arabia and East African coastal countries.

Trade object

North Korea, Japan, Okinawa, countries on the south central Peninsula, Southeast Asia, South Asia, the Islamic world, and parts of Europe. Export goods: Silk, tea, porcelain, gold, silver, books. Import goods: Glass, cat' s eye stone, pearl, ivory, spices, gold, silver, precious stones, crystal, agate, amber, camel skin, frankincense, myrrh, benzoin, incense, sandalwood, Lu Hui, pepper, wenatche and so on.

Significance

The Silk Road is a great invention in the history of civilization. It is the longest international transport routes between the ancient east and west, co-created by multi-ethnic along the road, so known as the way of friendship. The Silk Road made a significant contribution to the exchange of commodities, culture and religion.

Commodities exchange

Silk and porcelain became a symbol of East Asian powerful civilization. The heads of state and the nobles once took silk and porcelain as a symbol of wealth and glory. Besides, the Lapis Lazuli from Afghan also flowed in Europe and Asia. It was the symbol of wealth in Mesopotamia. When the lapis lazuli spread to India, where the Buddhists took it as one of the seven treasures of Buddhism, lapis lazuli add religious color forever.

The spread of grapes, walnuts, carrots, peppers, lima beans, spinach (also known as the Persian cuisine), cucumber, and pomegranates add more choices to East Asian people' s daily diet. Iron, gold, silver, out of the mirror and other luxury products were exported from China.

There are lots of mutual introduction and transplantation between the east and the west. Medicine, dance, martial arts and other famous animals and plants broaden their horizon. According to historical data, the government of Tang ever contacted with more than three hundred countries and regimes. Tens of thousands of guests from all over the world came to Chang' an every year.

Culture exchange "Diamond Sutra" of the Tang Dynasty, found in Dunhuang, is the oldest prints. It seems that only East Asian and South Asian countries have developed paper industry. As the open of the Silk Road, paper products began to appear in the western region and beyond. Paper of Second Century has been discovered in Kroraina. Although the Central Asian region also used paper, there was no evidence of the paper industry. Europe and Middle Asia experienced a huge change when paper came into the west. In the battle of Talas, the Arabs took Chinese prisoners of war back to Samarkand along the Silk Road. Some of them were paper craftsmen. Then paper has spread to all parts of the world.

The western region is covered by desert, so the prosperity of countries is inseparable from water. The melted snow from Tianshan and Kunlun Mountains is one of the main sources supplied for Western Regions. It was difficult to collect the melted snow, since it would evaporate or infiltrated into the ground. The Han troops developed agriculture in the western region, they also need Karez and Well and Canal to get water. Then the technology spread to more distant countries Gradually. It was a controversial issue at first. But it was confirmed in the Historical Records. When Li Guang beat Ferghana, they surround the city and cut off water for the city. But some people bored wells in the city.

Printing is another technology spread to the west along the Silk Road. "Diamond Sutra" of Tang is now preserved in the British, which shows that the printing has spread to Central Asia in the Tang Dynasty at least. In 13th century, Many European travelers came to China along the Silk Road and brought it back to Europe. In 15th century, Gutenberg printed the first "Bible" . In 1466, the first printing factory opened in Italy, so that the technology was quickly spread throughout Europe.

Religion exchange

After Buddhism was introduced into China in Han Dynasty, it began to spread in the North and South Dynasty. Then it became the Zen Buddhism in Chinese style. Buddhist culture has injected new blood for the development of China traditional philosophy and Neo Confucianism. The rhythm of Buddhism increased the rhythm of Chinese classical poetry. The contents enriched the vocabulary of Chinese language. Songyue Pagoda, Giant Wild Goose Pagoda, Famen Temple, Nanchan Temple, Foguang Temple, and Liuhe Pagoda are exquisite beyond compare, extraordinary as if done by the spirits. International friends all sighed for the view. These buildings absorbed the western architectural technology greatly. In the era of Emperor Taizong, Xuanzang (602-664) trave lled to ancient India for Buddhist scriptures. Great Tang Records on the Western Regions recorded India political, social and local customs. He got back 657 Buddhist classics. Giant Wild Goose Pagoda was built for collection and translation. Later, Yijing(602-664) travelled India again. He got back 400 Buddhist classics, introducing culture and life of South Asian countries to Chinese.

Nestorianism was introduced to China from Eastern Rome Empire in early Tang Dynasty. It had little impact. Manichaeism was introduced to China from Persia in mid-Tang Dynasty. It is believed that the light must conquer darkness, and that justice must be the root of evil, so that a lot of working people believe in it. The founder of Ming Dynasty was a follower. Islamism was introduced in Prime Tang. A lot of Mosques began to appear in Guangzhou, Chang' an and other places.

World heritage

In 22nd, June 2014, the thirty-eighth World Heritage Conference announced, "Silk Road: Changan - Tianshan corridor road network" was declared as World Cultural Heritage. It was the first successful example of multinational combined application for the World Cultural Heritage. The Silk Road project was included in the "World Heritage List", became thirty-second and thirty-third world cultural heritage in China

New Perspectives

From first exploration to the West Regimes to the development of the Silk Road, Chinese always share the great achievements of material civilization and spiritual civilization with the world. Chinese silk, tea, porcelain production technology, four great inventions and philosophers of classical theory were widely spread along the Silk Road, which promoted the continuation and development of world civilization. Meanwhile, western customs, habits, religious beliefs, and cultural products came into China along the Silk Road. They made progress and kept peace with mutual communication and study.

As the bridge between the ancient civilizations of East and West, the Silk Road promoted the mutual communication and cultural communication between different countries of Asia and Europe continent. It is not only a trade channel for material circulation, but also the bridge of humanity, religion, science and technology exchange between east and west. The Silk Road connected

Europe and Africc and Asia three continents, linked ancient Babylon, ancient Egypt, ancient India and ancient Chinese four ancient civilizations, Confucianism, Islam and Christianity three cultural circles. It promoted the interaction of human society, the nomadic hunting and fishing, farming and trade, marine and fusion. It promoted the formation of human destiny community, and made great contributions to the communication and development of human society.

Today, we follow our ancestors' steps to the west. We share the development of our material, cultural achievements and historical spirit wealth with the world in the rise of Chinese nation. It is not only a continuation of civilization, but also a continuation of national spirit blood. We should keep pace with the times, have courage to innovate and make efforts to pursue our dreams.

Zheng He's voyage to the western seas is an unprecedented feat in the history of navigation in the world. Therefore, Zheng He is considered to be the first messenger to the west in ancient China. However, according to the latest archaeological discoveries, the earliest Western diplomat was Yang Liangyao in the mid-Tang Dynasty. Yang Liangyao(736-806), born in Longyun. He was a eunuch.

In 756-758, Yang entered the court and began his legendary life with the identity of eunuch. In 785, he was ordered to travel to Dashi. He became first Chinese envoy to the Mediterranean coast. It has been 1230 yecrs since then. 620 years earlier than Zheng He. So we should not only be proud of Zheng He's great contribution to the world's maritime career, but also proud of Yang Liangyao's voyage to Middle Eastern early in the late eighth Century.

汉武帝运筹帷幄

Strategist Emperor Wu

汉武帝刘彻（公元前 156 年—公元前 87 年），西汉第七位皇帝，杰出的政治家、战略家、诗人，在政治清明、文化繁荣、国家稳定方面作出了不少贡献。军事上，他攘夷拓土、国威远扬，东并朝鲜、南吞百越、西征大宛、北破匈奴，奠定了汉地的基本范围，开创了汉武盛世的局面，另外他在开辟丝路、建立年号、颁布太初历、兴太学等方面也颇有建树。

在对抗匈奴的战争中，汉武帝运筹帷幄，在位期间同七代匈奴单于展开了半个世纪的军事斗争，兼用和平手段，使西域诸国臣服。后匈奴王庭远迁漠北，这就基本解决了自西汉初期以来匈奴对中原的威胁，为后来把西域并入中国版图奠定了基础。在公元前 133 年至 119 年期间，汉武帝派兵和匈奴进行了多次作战。其中决定性的战役有三次：河南之战、河西之战和漠北之战。

（一）河南之战

公元前 127 年（西汉元朔二年），匈奴左贤王部进犯上谷、渔阳。汉材官将军韩安国率 700 人出战，负伤败阵，退守壁垒不出，匈奴骑兵掳掠千余人及牲畜而去。汉武帝刘彻命韩安国部向东移驻右北平，以阻挡匈奴向东方深入，同时决定采取胡骑东进、汉骑西击的作战方针，令车骑将军卫青、将军李息急速出兵云中，突袭匈奴防

守薄弱的河南地。卫青、李息率部出塞后，从云中向西大迂回包抄，突然掩袭匈奴白羊王、楼烦王并一举击溃之，解除了长安的威胁。汉匈河南之战是汉匈战争史上一个重要的转折点，得益于河南地的收复，西汉王朝的北部边防线北推至黄河沿岸。役后，汉武帝在河南地置五原郡与朔方郡，并听从中大夫主父偃的建议，修筑朔方城，并招募十万内地居民至朔方实边。昔日匈奴刺向汉朝后背的利刃，迅速转变为汉军指向匈奴前胸的长戟。

（二）河西之战

公元前 121 年，汉武帝派霍去病出陇西，越过焉支山（甘肃山丹县东南胭脂山）西进，入匈奴境千余里，和其展开短兵肉搏，不但杀光了匈奴军的全部精锐，斩首八千九百六十级，还擒获了大量俘虏与辎重，可以说是大获全胜。同年夏天，霍去病第二次西征，越过居延泽（内蒙古居延海），攻到祁连山，大破匈奴军，歼敌 3 万余人，迫降单桓王、酋涂王及相国、都尉等 2500 人，俘虏 5 王及 5 王母、单于阏氏、王子 59 人，相国、将军、当户、都尉 63 人，使河西的匈奴贵族损失惨重。同年，匈奴贵族内部分裂，浑邪王率四万人降汉。这次战役后，西汉王朝完全占据了河西走廊地区，汉朝在这里置武威、酒泉、张掖、敦煌四郡，历史上称“河西四郡”，从此打开了通往西域的道路，切断了匈奴与羌人的联系，为日后向漠北的匈奴单于、左贤王部发动进攻创造了良好的条件。

（三）漠北之战

汉武帝元狩四年（公元前 119 年）的漠北战役，是汉军在距离中原最远的战场进行的一次规模最大任务也最艰巨的战役。此次战役是汉武帝向匈奴战略进攻的顶点，也是匈奴伊稚斜单于与西汉毕其功于一役的战略大决战。元狩四年初夏，汉武帝命卫青、霍去病各率五万骑兵远征漠北，又调集步兵数十万，民间私马四万匹，向前线运送军需物资，沿途保障。按照预定计划，卫青为右路，率各将出代郡，对匈奴左贤王实施歼灭性打击；骠骑将军霍去病为左路，率精骑五万出定襄，寻找伊稚斜单于主力决战。卫青、霍去病不负重托，充分领会了汉武帝的战略思想，每次出战都表现出主动进攻、大胆果决的进取精神，敢于快速冲击、远程奔袭、大范围迂回包围。由于他们的出色指挥，汉军跋涉千里而攻势不减，漠北之战最终以汉军的全面胜利而告终。此外，汉武帝在外交上派彭吴联络貊，以阻止匈奴向东发展，派张骞通西域，与西域诸国建立友好关系，以切断匈奴右臂；在经济上发展生产，实行盐铁官营、酒类专卖，整顿币制和税收等，都为打败匈奴提供了有利的条件。

在对战匈奴的各场战役当中，汉武帝运筹帷幄，从以往的作战经验中吸取教训，巧妙运用匈奴的麻痹心理，出其不意攻其不备，同时集中全国最精锐的骑兵和最优秀的战将投入战斗，并调集大批马匹与步兵，运送粮草辎重，以解决远距离作战的补给问题。与此同时，武帝识人善用，最大限度地发挥了统帅们的指挥才能，给与了匈奴前所未有的打击。汉武帝的雄图大略和正确决策，是西汉军队能够战胜匈奴的主要原因之一。

Liu Che (156B.C.-87B.C.), the seventh emperor in the Western Han Dynasty, a prominent politician, strategist, poet, has made great contributions to the political probity, cultural prosperity and national stability. Militarily speaking, he has conquered Korea、Baiyue、Ferghana and The Huns, laid the basic scope of the Han Dynasty, built a golden age of Emperor Wu. In addition, He has contributed a lot to creating the Silk Road, establishing regime era, promulgating Taichu Calendar and setting up Imperial College.

The emperor was anticipated and outsmarted in the fight against the Huns. He reigned with seven generations of the Huns khan for half a century of military struggle, combining peaceful means, and subjected the regimes in the western regions to its rule. Han and Xiongnu troops carried out many operations between 133B.C. and 119A.C. There were three decisive battles: the battle of Henan, the battle of the Hexi and the battle of MoBei.

1.the battle of Henan

In 127B.C., the Huns attacked on Shanggu, Yuyang. Han Anguo led 700 soldiers to the battle, failed and wounded, retreated in barriers. The Huns robbed thousands of slaves and livestock. The emperor commanded them to shift to Beiping, and decided to strike Henan, where The Huns' defense was weak. Wei Qing and Li Xi went out of the frontier pass, made a big outflanking from Yuzhong, and defeated the Huns. The battle of Henan was an important turning point. Thanks to recover Henan, the northern frontiers of the western Han Dynasty moved to the coast of the Yellow River. After the battle, the emperor set Wuyuan and Shuofang in Henan, and rebuilt Shuofang, recruiting hundreds of mainland residents to the north side. The Han Dynasty gained advantage again.

2.the battle of Hexi

In 121B.C., Huo Qubing and Han troops were engaged in hand-to-hand combat with the Huns. They not only killed all the elite of the Huns, but also captured a large number of prisoners and baggage. That is they made a clean sweep. In summer, Huo set out to Qilian Mountains for second expedition and beat the Huns again. They killed more than 30000 enemies, force 2500 leaders to surrender. The Hun nobles of Hexi region suffered heavy losses. In the same year, Xiongnu King Hunxie surrendered to the Han Dynasty with 40000 soldiers. After the campaign, the West Han Dynasty completely occupied the hexi corr'dor region. The Han Dynasty set four counties: Wuwei, Jiuquan, Zhangye and Dunhuang, called as "Four counties in Hexi Corridor" in history. Since then, The Han Dynasty has opened the way to the western regions, cut off the connection between Huns and Qiang, and created good condition for future attack.

3.the battle of Mobei

MoBei battle (119B.C.) was the most biggest and difficult battle, which is furthest from the central plains. It is the vertex of Han's strategic offensive and also the decisive battle between the Huns and the West Han Dynasty. In 119B.C.early summer, Wei Qing and Huo Qubing led the Han Army attack the Huns and won a total victory. In addition, the Han Dynasty established friendly relations with various western states, began to advance production energetically, which provided favorable conditions to defeat the Huns.

In all the battles to the Huns, The emperor strategized to achieve victory. He drawed lessons from past combats, applied the Huns psychological paralysis cleverly, and made surprise attack. Meanwhile, The emperor made good use of generals and maximize their brilliant generalship. Roughly and correct decisions of the emperor is one of the main causes for the Han Dynasty troops to defeat the Huns.

李广
Li Guang

马踏匈奴
Horse Stepping on a Xiongnu Soldier

李广（？—公元前 119 年），汉族，陇西成纪（今甘肃天水秦安县）人，中国西汉时期的名将。其先祖李信是秦朝名将，曾率军击败燕太子丹。李广家族世代接受仆射这一官职，世代传习射箭，因此李广的箭法十分精湛。《史记·李将军列传》中曾经记载了李广射石的故事：李广出猎，看到草丛中的一块石头，以为是老虎，张弓而射，一箭射去把整个箭头都射进了石头里。

李广将门出身，才气无双，被文帝与景帝所赏识。汉文帝十四年（公元前 166 年），匈奴大举入侵萧关，李广以良家子弟的身份从军抗击匈奴，因为精通骑马射箭，斩杀匈奴首级很多，被任为汉中郎。李广曾经随从皇帝出行，有冲锋陷阵抵御敌寇之功和与猛兽搏斗之勇，因而汉文帝说："可惜呀，你没遇到时机，假如让你生在高祖时代，封个万户侯不在话下！"汉景帝即位后，李广任陇西都尉，又改任骑郎将。武帝即位后，召李广为未央宫卫尉。元光六年（公元前 129 年），汉武帝遣李广、公孙敖、公孙贺和卫青四人率四万大军分别从雁门、云中、代郡、上谷四个方面同时出击入侵的匈奴军。李广任骁骑将军，领万余骑出击，因众寡悬殊负伤被俘。单于素闻李广有才，下令说："俘获李广定要活着送来。"匈奴骑兵便把他放在两匹马中间，装在绳编的网兜里躺着。李广佯装死去，斜眼看到旁边一个匈奴少年骑着一匹好马，便于途中趁隙跃起，跳马夺弓，向南飞驰数十里，重遇残部，便带领他们进入了边关要塞。没过多久，匈奴入侵杀死辽西太守，汉武帝命李广任右北平郡（治平刚县，今内蒙古宁城西南）太守。匈奴人敬畏李广的威名，称之为飞将军，数年不敢来犯。

然李广虽英勇善战，一生经历过大小七十多次战役，却始终时运不济，未能封侯。元狩四年（公元前 119 年），汉武帝发动漠北之战，由卫青、霍去病各率五万骑兵由定襄、代郡出击跨大漠远征匈奴本部，李广几次请求随行，汉武帝起初以他年老没有答应，后来经不起李广请求，同意他出任前将军，却暗中警告卫青，李广年老，命运不好，不能让他与单于对阵。在对战单于的过程中，卫青故意将李广调开，李广心中恼怒，不向卫青告辞就启程了。由于军队没有向导，李广迷失道路，未能参战，于是拔刀自刎，愤愧自杀。李广军中将士都为之痛哭。百姓听到这个消息，不论认识李广否，不论老少都为之落泪。

李广为将廉洁，对部下也很谦虚和蔼，常把自己的赏赐分给部下，与士兵同吃同饮，深得官兵爱戴。他做了四十多年俸禄二千石的官，家里没有多少多余的财物，也始终不谈购置家产的事。李广爱兵如子，凡事能身先士卒。行军遇到缺水断食之时，见水，见食，士兵不全喝到水，他不近水边；士兵不全吃遍，他不尝饭食。由于李广对士兵宽缓不苛，士兵们也甘愿为他出力卖命。司马迁曾夸赞："传曰'其身正，不令而行；其身不正，虽令不从'。其李将军之谓也？余睹李将军悛悛如鄙人，口不能道辞。及死之日，天下知与不知，皆为尽哀。彼其忠实心诚信于士大夫也？谚曰'桃李不言，下自成蹊'。此言虽小，可以谕大也。"

正因为李广的高洁人格和骁勇善战，其在后世人的文学作品中也常常以英勇将军的形象出现。唐朝诗人对李广多有赞颂。王昌龄在《出塞》中写道："秦时明月汉时关，万里长征人未还。但使龙城飞将在，不教胡马度阴山。"其中"飞将"即指"飞将军"李广。《滕王阁序》中说"冯唐易老，李广难封"，也是为飞将军不能封侯而感慨。卢纶在《塞下曲》中则描写李广射石的传奇故事："林暗草惊风，将军夜引弓。平明寻白羽，没在石棱中。" 边塞诗人高适也在《燕歌行并序》中写道："相看白刃血纷纷，死节从来岂顾勋。君不见沙场征战苦，至今犹忆李将军。"他感慨自己没有遇到像李广一样身先士卒、体恤将士的将军。由此可见，虽然李广未能像卫青、霍去病那样立功封侯，但是其高尚的情操和英勇的形象却始终为后人所尊敬和称道。

Li Guang (?-119 B.C.), Han, born in Chengji, Longxi, a famous general in the Western Han Dynasty. His ancestor Li Xin is a famous general of the Qin Dynasty, who once defeated Crown Prince Dan of Yan. Lee family is master of archery. "Historical Records Biography of General Li" recorded: Li Guang went hunting, drew and shot; the entire arrow was shot into the stone.

He was born in a military family with unrivalled talent and appreciated by Emperor Wen of Han and Emperor Jing of Han. In 166B.C.Xiong nu invaded Xiao Guan. Li Guang joined the army to beat against the Huns. Due to his proficient in horse and archery, killing countless, he was appointed as Zhong-Lang General of the Han Dynasty. Emperor Wen of Han ever said: "it' s a pity of you to be born at the wrong time. If you were born in the era of Emperor Gao, you would be in high position." In 129B.C, Li Guang, Gongsun Ao, Gongsun He and Wei Qing headed the troops attack the Huns in four different directions. Due to the disparity of numerical strength is too great, Li Guang and his army failed. Chanyu has long heard of Li Guang, he commanded to keep Li alive. Li pretended to die and seized the opportunity to escape. Feared of Li, the Huns did not dare to invade for several years.

Although General Li has experienced more than seventy campaigns in all his life, he did not get knighthoods official promotion. In 119B.C, the battle of Mobei began. General Li requested to join the fight for several times. Emperor Wu of Han refused at first, later he reluctantly agreed but dropped a warning of not let him be against Chanyu to Wei Qing. Knowing it, General Li was too angry to leave without saying goodbye. Li Guang got lost on the road and missed the battle. Then he felt ashamed and killed himself. Hearing the news, soldiers and ordinary people all shed tears for him.

General Li remained honest and clean. He was humble and kind to the soldiers, sharing awards with them. So he was loved by his soldiers. In forty-year official life, he never talked about the purchase of property. He loved his soldiers as his own sons, so the soldiers were also willing to devote themselves for him.

Sima Qian praised: "He, who is upright, acts without orders; He, who is coward, disobeys the orders." Li Guang did! General Li kept sincere and simple all his life. When he passed away, people of the country all felt sorry for him.

Li Guang often appeared in the literature of the world in the image of a brave general. Wang Changlin ever wrote: "The moon of Qin shines yet over the passes of Han; our men have not returned from the distant frontier. If the Winged General of Dragon City were there, no Hu horses could ever cross the Yinshan." The Winged General was General Li. Lu Lun ever wrote: "Woods dark and wind-startled grass, the general drew his bow at dusk. Searching the white feather in break of day, into the crack of a flint sunk the arrowhead." These poems show that Li Guang was respected and praised by future generations though he did not get high position like Weiqing and Huo Qubing.

凌烟阁二十四功臣

Twenty-four heroes of Ling Yange in Tang Dynasty

凌烟阁是唐朝为表彰功臣而建筑的绘有功臣图像的高阁，位于唐朝皇宫内三清殿旁的一个不起眼的小楼，后因“凌烟阁二十四功臣”而闻名于世。唐朝贞观十七年（公元643年）二月二十八日（3月23日），唐太宗李世民为了纪念和他一起打天下治天下的功臣，于是修建凌烟阁来陈列由阎立本所画的二十四位功臣的画像，即为《二十四功臣图》，比例为真人大小，面北而立，以示为臣之礼，并时常前往怀旧。阁中分为三层：最内一层所画均为功勋最高的宰辅之臣；中间一层所画均为功高王侯之臣；最外一层所画则为其他功臣。

李世民作为一位杰出的皇帝，不仅雄韬武略，文治武功，同时也很善于处理君臣之间的关系，恩威并施，双管齐下。设凌烟阁二十四元勋像就是其中一例。太宗一朝，君臣共同努力，结果出现了贞观盛世，为了表彰这些功臣，便命阎立本绘画《二十四功臣图》于凌烟阁。当时的李世民年迈体衰，开始怀念往事，追想当年金戈铁马气吞万里的战斗岁月。于是就将他那些老部下的形象绘入凌烟阁，以为人臣荣耀之最，此后凌烟阁功臣成为唐代豪杰从军报国功成名就的标志。

这二十四位功臣分别是：左武卫大将军长孙无忌、监校千牛卫大将军李孝恭、左仆射杜如晦、谏议大夫魏徵、右仆射房玄龄、尚书高士廉、尚书尉迟敬德、鹤城太守李靖、尚书令萧瑀、护国将军段志玄、尚书刘弘基、洛阳郡守屈突通、荆州长史殷开山、右武卫上将军柴绍、京兆尹长孙顺德、洛州长史张亮、扬州郡守侯君集、武威长史张公谨、虎贲将军程知节、尚书虞世南、左令刘政会、右令唐俭、上将军李勣和虎威将军秦琼。李贺的《南园十三首》有诗为证：“男儿何不带吴钩，收取关山五十州。请君暂上凌烟阁，若个书生万户侯。”

这二十四位功臣为李世民立下汗马功劳，为贞观之治作出了杰出的贡献。然而随着盛世的出现，功臣们各自的命运遭际也各不相同。谋臣杜如晦房玄龄勤勤恳恳，小心翼翼，尽心竭力病故而亡；宗室名王李孝恭独称军功，战功几可与李世民分庭抗礼，太宗登基后，便退出权力中心，封河间郡王以歌舞美人自娱；尉迟敬德在玄武门之变中拥立之功第一，后攻打突厥有功，天下安定后无用武之地，晚年闭门不出，最终得享天年；李靖善于明哲保身，故而终生无大患，但在由于在玄武门之变中保持中立，且军事能力过高遭人疑忌，屡次被诬告谋反，为免嫌疑，主动退休闭门不出；长孙顺德在太原起兵时立有大功，但最终晚节不保，贞观年间因多次贪污被弹劾，李世民不忍治罪，只贬官而已；张亮出身寒贱，外恭内诡，官至刑部尚书且参知政事，却养五百义子意图不轨，最终被处斩；侯君集摧凶克敌，恃宠矜功，曾助李靖击败吐谷浑，又任主将击灭高昌，却因私吞高昌战利品而被弹劾，后在李世民诸子争当太子的斗争中，依附太子李承乾，图谋杀李世民，最终事泄被杀……在中国最辉煌朝代的盛世中，一朝功臣最终汇入历史长河，他们的功过，也都交由后人去评说。

Ling Yange is the place to commend persons who have rendered meritorious for their service. It is located in the Palace of Chang' an City, beside Sanqing Hall, known as "Twenty-four Heroes of Ling Yange" . In March 23, Tang Zhengguan seventeen years (643A.D.), Tang Taizong Li Shimin built Ling Yange to display the great character portraits, painted by Yan Liben, in memory of the heroes who conquer and rule the world with him. The portraits are in real size; face to the North, which shows respects to the Emperor. The cabinet is divided into three layers: prime ministers' portraits are in the inside layer; nobility' s portraits are in the middle layer; the other heroes' are in the outside layer.

Li Shimin was an outstanding Emperor. He had extraordinary talent and strategy, made remarkable administrative and military achievements. He took the policy of incentives and penalties and made a harmonious relationship with the ministers. Setting up twenty-four great character portraits in Ling Yange is an example. At the beginning of Tang, the Zhenguan rulers and the ministers strived together to accomplish "governing of the Zhenguan magnificent" . So the Emperor commanded Yan Liben to paint "image of twenty-four heroes" in Ling Yange. Li Shimin was old and frail at that time; he began to look back upon the years of fighting. Therefore Ling Yange Hero became the symbol of the hero who serves the motherland successfully in Tang Dynasty.

Twenty-four heroes of Ling Yange are Zhangsun Wuji, Li Xiaogong, Du Ruhui, Wei Zheng, Fang Xuanlin, Gao Shilian, Yuchi Jingde, Li Jing, Xiao Yu, Duan Zhixuan, Liu Hongji, Qu Tutong, Yin Kaishan, Chai Shao, Zhangsun Shunde, Zhang Liang, Hou Junji, Zhang Gongjin, Cheng Zhijie, Yu Shinan, Liu Zhenghui, Tang Jian, Li Ji, Qin Qiong.

Twenty-four heroes have rendered meritorious for Li Shimin and have made outstanding contribution to "governing of the Zhenguan magnificent" . However, as the emergence of the flourishing age, their destinies are different from each other. Famous adviser Du Ruhui and Fang Xuanlin worked diligently and carefully until died of illness. The military exploit of Lord Li Xiaogong was able to stand up to Li Shimin' s. He stepped back from the power center when Li became King. Yuchi Jingde distinguished himself in Incident at Xuanwu Gate, and then attacked the Turks. In later life, he kept at home, finally had died of old age. Li Jing was always worldly wise and played safe. But he was wrongly accused of rebellion several times because of his military capability and neutral attitude in Incident at Xuanwu Gate. So he chose to retire. Zhangsun Shunde made contributions in Taiyuan. But he was impeached owing to graft during Zhengguan period so that banished from the court. Zhangliang was born into a poor family. He complied in public but opposed in private. He adopted 500 sons to hatch a sinister plot, finally killed by the Emperor. Hou Junji was haughty because of his distinguished service in the battle and the Emperor' s trust. In the fight for crown prince, he attached Prince Li Chengqian, and tried to murder Li Shimin. At last, he was killed as things were brought to light. In the most brilliant Dynasty of China, a generation of Heroes would be recorded in history. Their merits or faults need to be comment by future generations.

唐太宗李世民與凌烟閣二十四功臣諸像

昭君出塞

Zhaojun Departs the Frontier

昭君出塞 Zhaojun Departs the Frontier

昭君出塞（约公元前 52 年—约前 15 年），名嫱，字昭君，汉族，南郡秭归（今湖北省宜昌市兴山县）人，与貂蝉、西施、杨玉环并称中国古代四大美女。王昭君出生于南郡秭归（今湖北兴山县）的一户平民之家，汉元帝建昭元年（公元前 38 年），以民间女子的身份被选入掖庭，成为了一名宫女。

竟宁元年（公元前 33 年）正月，时为匈奴单于的呼韩邪第三次朝汉自请为婿，元帝遂将昭君赐给了呼韩邪单于，并改元为竟宁。单于非常高兴，上书表示愿意永保塞上边境。公元前 33 年昭君抵达匈奴，被称为宁胡阏氏。昭君和呼韩邪单于共同生活了三年，生下一子，取名伊屠智伢师，封右日逐王。建始二年（公元前 31 年），呼韩邪单于去世，大阏氏之子雕陶莫皋被立为复株累单于。依照匈奴婚俗，父死，子可以娶后母，昭君迫于大局，忍受着极大的委屈，又嫁给了复株累单于。（据《后汉书》记载，呼韩邪单于死后，复株累单于想娶昭君为妻。昭君上书汉成帝，请求返回中原，成帝拒绝了她的请求，敕令昭君遵从匈奴习俗。）昭君与复株累单于共同生活了十一年，生有二女，长女名须卜居次，次女名当于居次。但昭君的悲剧并未到此为止，鸿嘉元年（公元前 20 年），复株累单于去世，且麋胥继任为搜谐若鞮单于。她又被命嫁给新单于，复株累的长子，也就是呼韩邪的孙子，昭君终于承受不住，彻底崩溃了，她最后选择了服毒自尽。一代佳人就此香消玉殒，命断异乡，空留下一方青冢在阴山脚下、大漠深处，遥望着南方的故国。泰始二年（公元 266 年），司马炎称帝，建立西晋，追尊司马昭为文帝，为避司马昭的讳，王昭君被改称明君，史称“明妃”。

昭君出塞，为边塞和平、民族团结和文化交流作出了重要贡献。

（一）对于边塞和平的贡献

昭君出塞后的几十年时间里，汉匈两家一直保持了友好和睦关系，因此西汉末年的和亲是成功的。西汉呼韩邪单于附汉与昭君出塞，不但结束了匈奴多年的分裂和战乱，而且为中原王朝的大一统奠定了基础。此外，和亲的方式加强了汉匈双方的交流，使当时相对落后的少数民族产生了对中原先进制度的向往，促使一些少数民族效仿中原的制度。

（二）对于民族团结的贡献

昭君出塞后，劝阻呼韩邪单于不要发动战争，还把中原的文化传给匈奴。从此，汉匈两族团结和睦，国泰民安，“边城晏闭，牛马布野，三世无犬吠之警，黎庶忘干戈之役”，展现出欣欣向荣的和平景象。王昭君为实现汉朝与匈奴的和睦相处而远嫁匈奴，开创了汉匈间 60 年无战事的和平局面。昭君使汉朝与匈奴和好，边塞的烽烟熄灭了 50 年，加强了汉族与匈奴民族之间的民族团结，符合汉族和匈奴族人民的利益。她与她的子女后孙以及姻亲们对胡汉两族人民的和睦亲善与团结做出了巨大贡献，从客观上缓解了汉朝与匈奴的关系。元代诗人赵介认为，王昭君的功劳，不亚于汉朝名将霍去病。昭君的故事，成为了我国历史上流传不衰的民族团结的佳话。她不仅有惊人的美丽，而且负有替汉家君王传播光明、和番宁胡的重大使命。

李白曾作诗慨叹王昭君的事迹：“昭君拂玉鞍，上马啼红颜。今日汉宫人，明朝胡地妾。汉家秦地月，流影照明妃。一上玉关道，天涯去不归。”王昭君作为一代佳人，牺牲了个人的自由，远离家乡，远嫁匈奴，为汉匈和平做出了巨大的贡献，成就了民族团结的佳话。然而，这对历史来说是传奇，对王昭君个人来说却是一出伟大的悲剧。昭君以个人的幸福换来了边塞的和平，加强了双方的文化交流，她是不幸的，又是伟大的。她美丽而坚强的形象将一直在后人心中流传。也正因为如此，王昭君的故事在民间流传甚广，诗、词、小说、戏曲创作亦多以其为题材。据统计，古往今来反映王昭君的诗歌有七百多首，与之有关的戏曲、小说近四十种，写过昭君事迹的著名作者有五百多人。

Wang Zhaojun (52B.C-15B.C), Han, born in Zigui (today Yichang, Hubei). DIAO Chan, XI Shi, Yang Yuhuan and she are generally regarded as the four major ancient Chinese beauties. Wang Zhaojun was born in an ordinary family. In 38B.C, she was elected to the court as a maid.

In the first month of 33B.C, Emperor Yuan ordered Zhaojun marry to Huhanye Chanyu and designed reign title as Jingning. Chanyu was so pleased that he promised to keep peace forever. In 33B.C, Zhaojun arrived Xiongnu, called as Yan Zhi. Zhaojun and Huhanye Chanyu lived together for three years and gave birth to a son. In 31B.C, Huhanye Chanyu passed away, his son Diaotiaomohao was chosen as Fuzhulei Chanyu. According to the customs, the father died, the son can marry stepmother. Under the overall situation, Zhaojun had to marry him. They lived together for eleven years and h ad two daughters. However, the tragedy did not end here. In 20B.C, Fuzhulei Chanyu passed away. His son inherited. Zhaojun was ordered to marry Chanyu again. She committed suicide after her husband' s death as her only resort in order to avoid marrying her son. A beauty passed away, leaving a grave under Mountain Yin, deep in the desert. In 266, Sima Yan established the West Jin Dynasty. He honored Sima Zhao as Emperor Wen, Zhaojun as Ming Jun that is Ming Fei in history.

Lady Zhao jun, made an important contribution to the peace of frontier, national unity and cultural exchanges.

1. The peace of frontier

After Zhaojun departed the frontier, Han and Xiongnu have kept peace for more than ten years. So it was successful to make peace with rulers of Xiongnu by marriage in the late west Han Dynasty. The marriage not only ended the division and conflict with Xiongnu, but made a solid foundation for the unity of China.

2. National unity

Zhaojun persuaded Chanyu not to start a war, and spreaded the culture of the Central Plains to the Huns. Since then, two nations have kept peace and prosperity. To realize the harmony and peace between two nations, Wang Zhaojun married the Huns. There have been no wars for sixty years. The marriage accorded with the aspirations of the people. She and her children have made great contributions to releasing the relationship of Han and Hu and keeping harmony and friendly. Zhao Jie, a poet of Yuan Dynasty, thought Wang Zhaojun' s contribution was no less than Huo Qubing' s in Han Dynasty. The story of Zhaojun became popular story of national unity in Chinese history. Besides amazing beauty, she also took important mission of spreading sunshine and peace for the Chinese king.

As a beautiful lady, Wang Zhaojun gave up her own freedom and left home for Xiongnu. It may a legend in history. But it was a great tragedy of Zhaojun. She was unfortunate, but great. Her beautiful and strong image will influence later generations. Thus, her story continues to circulate. Lost of literatures ever chose Zhao Jun as the subjects.

法显求经

Fa xian traveled for Budhist scriptures

法显（公元 334 年—420 年），东晋司州平阳郡武阳（今山西临汾地区）人，一说是并州上党郡襄垣（今山西襄垣）人。作为中国佛教史上的一位名僧，一位卓越的佛教革新人物，法显是中国第一位到海外取经求法的大师，杰出的旅行家和翻译家。

法显本姓龚，他有三个哥哥，都在童年夭亡，他的父母担心他也夭折，在他才三岁的时候，就把他度为沙弥。十岁时，父亲去世。他的叔父考虑到他的母亲寡居难以生活，便要他还俗。法显这时对佛教的信仰已非常虔诚，他对叔父说："我本来不是因为有父亲而出家的，正是要远尘离俗才入了道。"他的叔父也没有勉强他。不久，他的母亲也去世了，他回去办理完丧事仍即还寺。二十岁时，法显受比丘戒（和尚进入成年后，为防止身心过失而履行的一种仪式）。从此，他对佛教信仰之心更加坚贞，行为更加严谨，时有"志行明敏，仪轨整肃"之称誉。东晋安帝隆安三年（399 年），法显和同学慧景、道整、慧应、慧嵬等前往天竺求法，从长安出发，遍历北、西、中、东天竺仲，获《方等般泥洹经》、《摩诃僧祇律》、《萨婆多律抄》、《杂阿毗昙心论》、《摩诃阿毗昙》等梵本，后又在师子国（今斯里兰卡）获《弥沙塞律》、《长阿含》及《杂藏》等梵本，前后历时 14 年，于义熙九年归国。

佛教从印度传入中国，到了法显时代，已经达到了一个关键时刻，一个转折点，从过去的基本上是送进来的阶段向拿进来的阶段转变。当时佛教在中国流传的内容主要有两大体系，一是以支谶、支谦为代表的大乘空宗般若学；一是以安世高为代表的小乘禅学。一个外来的宗教，传入一个文化传统迥异的国家，不可避免地要发生冲撞，佛教也不能例外。经过相当长时间的试探、伪装、适应，到了东晋时期，佛教逐渐为中国人所接受，最后达到了融合的阶段。晋末宋初的西行求法运动，就是在这样的情况下兴起来的。根据汤用彤先生的《汉魏两晋南北朝佛教史》的统计，西行求法活动自朱士行而后，以晋末宋初为最盛。而在所有这些西行求法者中，法显无疑是最突出的一个。这里所谓"突出"，归纳起来约略表现在以下几个方面：（一）法显旅行所到之地最多、最远；（二）法显真正到了印度；（三）法显携归翻译的戒律起了作用；（四）法显对大乘教义发展和顿悟学说的兴起起了很大的作用。

法显的功绩主要在于取经和翻译。他携归和翻译的经历代经录都有著录，但是他写的《法显传》对于世界的影响却远远超过了他的翻译对于中国的影响。《法显传》在历代著录中有很多不同的名称，比如《佛游天竺记》、《释法显行传》、《历游天竺记》、《佛国记》、《历游天竺记传》、《释法显游天竺记》、《佛游天竺本记》、《释法明游天竺记》、《法明游天竺记》、《历游天竺记传》、《法显记》等等，名称固繁，版本亦多。《法显传》在国际上的影响，首先表现在它的外文译本之多上。根据章巽的统计，共有英译本三，译者为 Samuel Beal（1869）、James Legge（1886）和 H.A.Giles（1923）；日译本三，译者为足立喜六:《考证法显传》（1935）、《法显传——中亚、印度、南海纪行研究》（1940）和长泽和俊（1970）。既然有了这样多的译本，那就必然有相应多的影响。而在这当中，《法显传》对印度的影响尤为巨大。众所周知，印度古代缺少真正的史籍，这一点马克思曾指出过。因此，研究印度古代历史，必须依靠外国的一些著作，其中尤以中国古代典籍最为重要，而在这些典籍中，古代僧人的游记更为突出。僧人游记数量极多，而繁简不同，时代先后也不一致。《法显传》是最古的和最全的之一。一向被认为与唐玄奘的《大唐西域记》和义净的《大唐西域求法高僧传》、《南海寄归内法传》鼎足而三。研究印度古代史的学者，包括印度学者在内，都视之为瑰宝。有一位著名的印度史学家曾写信说："如果没有法显、玄奘和马欢的著作，重建印度历史是不可能的。" 作为中国佛教史上的名僧，法显不仅为中国佛教的发展作出了重大贡献，更为佛教的跨域交流，为中印历史的传承记录下了光辉灿烂的一笔。

法显求经 Fa xian traveled for Budhist scriptures

Faxian (334A.D.—420A.D.) , born in Shanxi Linfen in Eastern Jin Dynasty. As a famous Buddhist in the history of Chinese Buddhism and an outstanding Buddhist innovator, Faxian is the first master to go on a pilgrimage for Buddhist scriptures overseas, he is also an outstanding traveler and translator.

Faxian' s family name is Gong. He has three brothers, who died young. Worried about his health, his parents let him go to the temple as a novice when he was three years old. At the age of ten, he lost his father. Considering it was difficult to live for his widowed mother, his uncle suggested him should resume secular life. However, his belief in Buddhism has been very religious at that time, he said, "I entered monastic life to stay away from the secular , not for my father." His uncle didn' t force him. Soon afterwards, his mother passed away. He went back to the temple after completing the funeral. Faxian was initiated into monkhood at the age of twenty. Then, He became more faithful to the Buddhist and his behavior became more serious. In 339A.D, Faxian went on a pilgrimage to Tenjiku for Buddhist scriptures with his friends Huijing, Daozheng, Huiying, and Huiwei. They traveled north, west, middle, east of Tenjiku from Chang' an for 14 years, and got back in 413A.D.They got several Sanskrit version of the sutra.

In the era of Faxian, Buddhism has reached a critical moment in China. There was a distinct change from "come" to "take" . There were two main contents of Buddhism in China. One was Mahayana Buddhism , the other was Theravada Buddhism. A foreign religion passed in a country of different culture, it is inevitable to have a collision, and Buddhism is no exception. After quite a long time of temptation, camouflage and adaptation, Buddhism gradually accepted by Chinese, finally reached the fusion stage in Eastern Jin Dynasty. West religion movement rose in such cases in Late Jin Dynasty and early Song Dynasty. According to Mr. Shang Yongtong, Faxian was the most prominent one among those who go the west for Buddhist scriptures. It mainly shows as the following: 1.Faxian traveled most and farthest; 2.Faxian reached India truly; 3. The religious discipline he translated has taken effect; 4.he made a contribution to the rise of Mahayana doctrine and Satori.

His achievement mainly lies in the scriptures and the translation. However, the Biography of Faxian has far more impact on the world than the influence of his translation on China. The Biography of Faxian has many different names in past ages of the woodblock. It has many different names and versions. There are a lot of foreign language versions in the world. According to Mr.Zhang Xun, there are three English versions, translated by Samuel Beal (1869) 、James Legge (1886) and H.A.Giles (1923) ; Japanese versions, two of them translated by ADACHI KIROKU, the other translated by Nagasawa Kazutoshi. Since there are so many versions, there must be a corresponding impact.

The Biography of Faxian has particular impact on India. As everyone knows, ancient India lacks real historical records, which pointed out by Marx. To study the ancient history of India, we must rely on some foreign works, among which the most important one is Chinese works. And the travel notes of ancient monks are the most prominent. There are quite a lot of travel notes with different detailing degrees in different times. The Biography of Faxian is one of the oldest and the most complete. The scholar who specialized in ancient India, including India scholars, all treat it as treasures. A famous India historian ever said, "It is impossible to rebuilt India history without the works of Faxian, Xuanzang and Mahuan." As a famous monk in the history of Chinese Buddhism, Faxian not only made contributions to Chinese Buddhism, but also facilitating with Buddhism exchanges in different areas.

圣僧玄奘
The holy man Xuan Zang

圣僧唐玄奘

The holy man Xuan Zang of the Tang Dynasty

西行求经 For westbound Buddhist scriptures

求经路上 On the way to seek

学成那烂陀寺 Complete the study in Nalanda

三藏法师讲译图 In the Tipiwakqcariya of Scripture about the Tripitaka master

載誉而归
大唐三藏聖教序
太宗文皇帝製
盖聞二儀有象顯覆載以含生四時無形潛寒暑以
太宗文皇帝製
弘福寺沙門懷仁集晉右將軍王羲之書
盖聞二儀有像顯

载誉而归 Full of glory and return

万世景仰 Eternal admiration

玄奘（公元 602 年 ~664 年），唐代著名高僧，法相宗创始人，洛州缑氏（今河南洛阳偃师）人，其先颍川人。其俗家姓名为“陈祎”，“玄奘”是其法名，被尊称为“三藏法师”，后世俗称“唐僧”，与鸠摩罗什、真谛并称为中国佛教三大翻译家。

玄奘是东汉名臣陈寔的后代，曾祖父陈钦，曾任后魏上党太守；祖父陈康，以学优出仕北齐，任国子博士，食邑周南（河南洛阳）；父亲陈惠，为时人之所景仰，曾做江陵的县官，后来隋朝衰亡，便隐居乡间、托病不出，当时的有识之士都称赞他的志节。陈惠共生四子，玄奘是他的第四个儿子。幼年跟父亲学《孝经》等儒家典籍，“备通经典”，“爱古尚贤”，养成了良好的品德。父亲云世后，其二兄陈素在洛阳净土寺出家，即长捷法师。玄奘十一岁那年，便随长捷入寺受学《法华经》、《维摩经》等。其后迁蜀，通过众多名师的指授，玄奘对“大小乘经论”，“南北地论”、“摄论学说”等均有了甚深的见地，闻名蜀中。

佛教学术界在“一阐提众生有无佛性”上一直存在着论争。到了玄奘的时代，北方流行已久的《涅槃经》、《成实经》、《毗昙》学与真谛在南方译传的《摄论》、《俱舍论》，构成当时南北佛学的主流。但玄奘师通过学习，深感真谛等古德译著不善，致使义理含混，理解不一，注疏也不同，对一些重要的理论问题分歧很大，难以融合。为探究佛教各派学说分歧，因此他于贞观元年，一人西行五万里，历经艰辛到达印度佛教中心那烂陀寺取真经。经过十七年，学遍了当时的大小乘各种学说。唐贞观十九年（公元 645 年），46 岁的玄奘自印度归国，共带回佛舍利 150 粒、佛像 7 尊、经论 657 部。在此后的 20 年中，他把全部的心血和智慧奉献给了译经事业。在长安和洛阳两地，玄奘在助手们的帮助下，共译出佛教经论 74 部，1335 卷，每卷万字左右，合计 1335 万字，占去整个唐代译经总数的一半以上，相当于中国历史上另外三大翻译家译经总数的一倍多，而且在质量上大大超越前人，成为翻译史上的杰出典范。玄奘的译典著作有《大般若经》、《心经》、《解深密经》、《瑜伽师地论》、《成唯识论》等。其西行实录《大唐西域记》共有十二卷，记述了他西游亲身经历的 110 个国家及传闻的 28 个国家的山川、地邑、物产、习俗等。中国古典名著《西游记》即以其取经事迹为原型。

玄奘是研究中国传统佛教成就最大的学者之一，又是继承印度正统佛教学说的集大成者。他不顾艰难困苦，万里迢迢去天竺寻求佛法，并发展了自己的几种主要学说如五种姓说、唯识哲学、因明学等，以搜集到的大量佛教典籍深刻地影响了东亚文化（包括中国文化、韩国文化和日本文化）的发展，同时也为东亚文化能在世界文化中发挥积极作用打下了基础。与此同时，在中国译经史上，玄奘结束了一个旧时代，开辟了一个新时代。从东汉至魏晋南北朝时期，中外翻译家对于译经各有贡献，但从总体上说，玄奘的成就都在他们之上。印度佛学从弥勒、无著、世亲，次第相承，直到陈那、护法、戒贤等人，已定为因明、对法、戒律、中观和瑜伽五科。玄奘的翻译工作，在中印文化交流史上，无疑起到了相互了解、相互学习的作用。

玄奘被世界人民誉为中外文化交流的杰出使者，其爱国及护持佛法的精神，被誉为“中华民族的脊梁”。他对中国文化的发展所做的贡献是多方面的，其中最伟大的是他对佛学典籍的翻译。他以不畏生死的精神，西行取佛经，并将全部的心血和智慧奉献给了译经事业，促进了佛学的跨域交流，体现了大乘佛法渡化众生的理念，为佛教的传承做出了重要的贡献。他的足迹遍布印度，影响远至日本、韩国以至全世界。他的思想与精神如今已是中国、亚洲乃至世界人民的共同财富。

Xuánzàng (602A.D.~ 664A.D.) is a famous monk in Tang Dynasty, the founder of Budd. School, born in Henan Luoyang; ancestral home in Yingchuan. He is formerly known as Chen Hui, whose Dharma name is Xuánzàng, honored as "Tripitaka" , also called as "Tang Monk" , with Kumārajīva and paramārtha known as Chinese three Buddhist translators.

Xuánzàng is the descendant of Chen Shi, who is famous minister in the Eastern Han Dynasty; his great-grandfather is Chen Qin, Shangdang Prefecture of Hou Wei Dynasty; his grandfather is Chen Kang, Country doctor of Bei Qi Dynasty, whose fief is Henan Luoyang; his father is Chen Hui, county officer in Jiangling. As the decline of Sui Dynasty, he lived in seclusion, respected by local people. Chen Hui has four sons, whose forth son is Xuánzàng. Xuánzàng studied "The Book of Filial Piety" and other Confucian classics from his father when he was young. He was proficient in Confucian classics, respected noble-minded people, and then developed a good moral character. His second brother, Changjie Mock, became a mock in Luoyang Jingtu Temple after his father died. When Xuánzàng was eleven, he learned Lotus Sutra, Vimalakirti-nirdesa-sutra from Changjie Mock. When moved to Sichuan, he learned from various famous teachers, then had eminent good sense in "The Mahayana Buddhism and The Hinayana Buddhism" , "The South and North Dilun School" , and "Shelun School" . So he was famous in inner Sichuan.

Whether all living creatures have Buddha-nature remains a controversial issue in Buddhist academic circle. By the time of Xuánzàng, Nirvana Sutra, Chengshi Sutra and Abhidharma, which had been popular in the north, and Shelun, Jushelun, disseminated by paramārtha in the south, had become the mainstream of Northern and Southern Buddhism. However, Xuánzàng felt bad about their translation works, which led to ambiguous philology, different explanation and misunderstanding of some important theoretical issues. And it was difficult to explore the differences of these Buddhism doctrines. 627A.D. he went to India Buddhist Centre , Nalanda Temple, to acquire scriptures. After seventeen years, he learned all kinds of theories. Tang Zhenguan nineteen years (645A.D.) , Xuánzàng came back to Chang' an, with 45 Buddhist relics, 7 Buddha statues, and 657 classics. In the next 20 years, he devoted himself to sutra translation. In Luoyang and Chang' an, with the help of the assistants, he translated 74 classics, including 1335 volumes, a thousand words per volume, a total of 1335 words, accounted for more than half of the total number of translated versions of the Tang Dynasty, equivalent to more than twice the sum of other three translators, he is an outstanding example of the history of translation. Xuánzàng has translated "Prajnaparamita Sutra" , "Heart Sutra" , "Sandhinirmocana Sutra" , "Yogacara-bhumi-sastra" , "Chen Wei-Shih Lun" and so on. 12 volumes of "Great Tang Records on the Western Regions" records the mountains, rivers, cities, products and custom in 110 counties he ever traveled and 28 countries he ever heard. His experience became the prototype of Chinese classical novels "Journey to the West" .

Xuánzàng is one of the greatest achievements in the study of Chinese traditional Buddhism, and the master of India orthodox Buddhist doctrine. He developed several doctrines, such as panca-gotrāni, idealism, Hetuvidya. His collection of Buddhist classics has a profound impact on the development of East Asian culture (including Chinese culture, Korean culture and Japanese Culture), and also laid the foundation for the East Asian culture to play an active role in the world culture. Meanwhile, In Chinese Buddhist translation history, Xuánzàng ended an old era, opened up a new era. General, Xuánzàng won the greatest achievements during the period of Eastern Han Dynasty to Wei Jin and southern and Northern Dynasties. India Buddhism passed from Maitreya，Asanga，Vasabandhu to Dignāga, Shilabhadra. They have set for five subjects. There is no doubt that Xuánzàng' s translations promote cultural exchanges between China and India.

Xuánzàng is honored as an outstanding Ambassador of Chinese and foreign cultural exchange. Due to his spirit of patriotism and Dharma, he is known as "the backbone of the Chinese nation". His contribution to the development of Chinese culture is various; the most important is his transitional Buddhist translation. He went to India for Buddhist sutras，ignoring all matters concerning his own life and death, and devoted himself to sutra translation, promoted the exchange of Buddhism in different areas, which embodied the concept of Mahayana Buddhism to sentient beings, and made an important contribution to the inheritance of Buddhism. He has travelled extensively in India, made influence in Japan, South Korea and even all over the world. His mind and spirit are the common wealth of the people of China, Asia and even the world.

大唐西市
Tang West Market

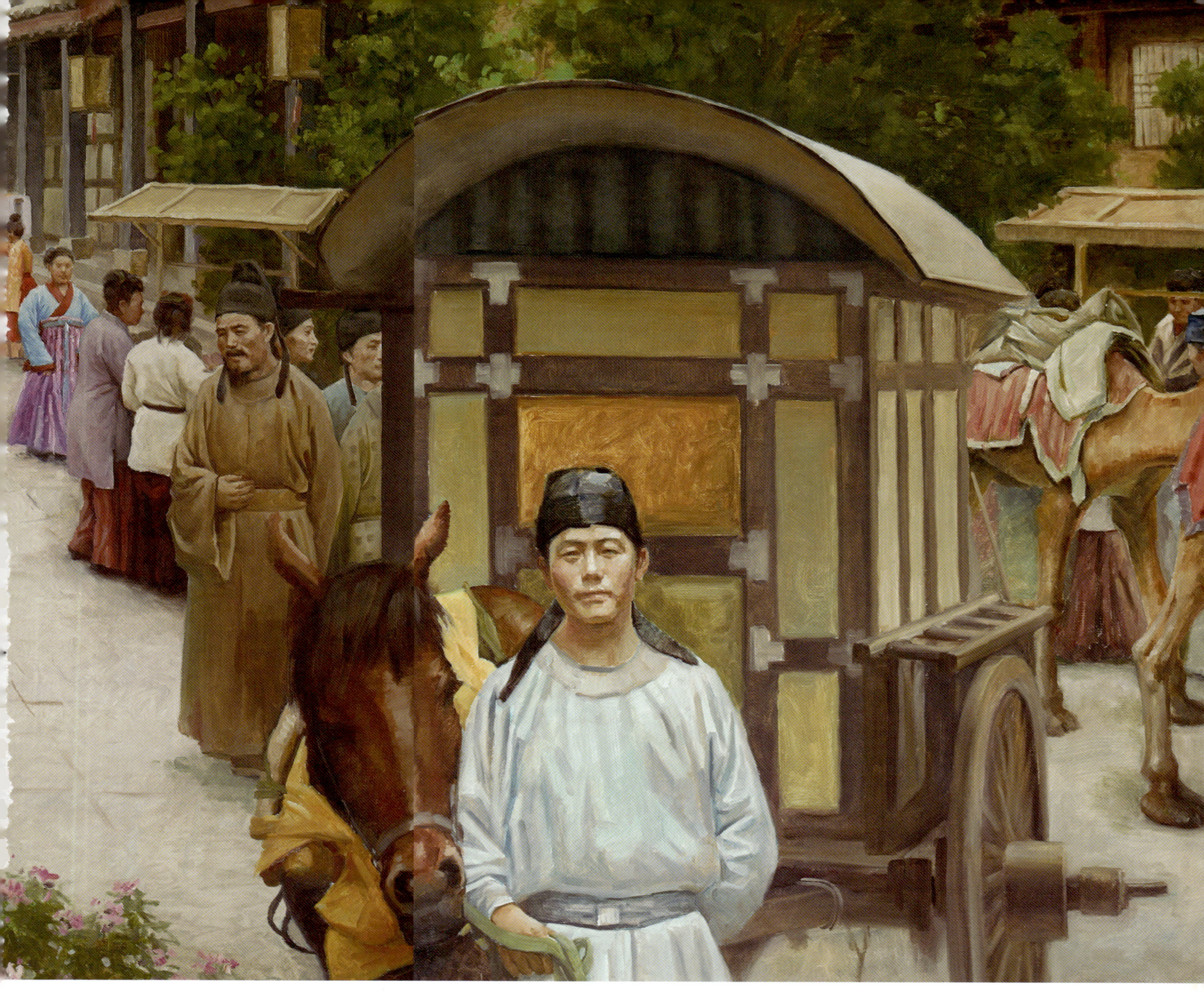

西市位于唐长安皇城的西南方（即今天的劳动南路和东桃园村之间），始建于隋（公元581年—617年），兴盛于唐（公元618年—907年），占地1600亩，建筑面积100多万平方米，有220多个行业，繁华程度盛极一时。唐长安实行比较严格的坊市制，居住区“坊”与经济区“市”互不干扰，体现着社会分层秩序和律令社会形态。东市在朱雀大街之东第三街，西市在朱雀大家之西第三街。唐长安的西市跟里坊一样，四周皆有高大的围墙，宋敏求《长安志》等记载其规模相当庞大，每个市约占2个坊的面积，市内有4条大街，围墙四面各有2个门，这在对西市遗址进行全面勘察与测量时得到证实。作为长安城乃至全国最主要的市场，西市进行的是封闭式的集中交易，也就是将若干个同类的商品聚集起来，以“肆”（或相当的“行”、“店”）为单位组成的，市内设有专门的管理机构。

根据考古发掘成果，西市遗址平面呈长方形，南北1031米，东西927米，面积0.96平方公里，其范围在今西安莲湖区东桃园以东、老糜家桥以西、东桃园桥以北、中国航空器材公司西北分公司以南，先劳南市场位置。发掘时，西市的北面、东面尚有夯筑的围墙基址，墙基皆宽4米多。西市内有南北向和东西向均宽16米的平等街道各两条，四街纵横交叉“井”字形，将整个市内划分成9个长方形区域，其中东

大唐西市 Tang West Market

West Market in Chang' an was bustling and flourishing before the late Tang Dynasty, an open public area for the courts political life and ordinary people' s daily life, an indispensable urban economic region from emperor down to folks inside and outside Chang' an city, a city window opened to the closed old city in Mediaeval Times of China. West Market was one of economic activity center in Chang' an city, (the other is East Market), the national industrial and commercial trade center, an important place for economic exchange between China and other counties, and a window to display the material progress of the glorious Tang Dynasty and the Silk Road civilization. There are various merchants, inns, goods and traders in West Market. As an urban economic region for the greatest amount of currency in circulation and the greatest sales volume in the world, West Market has played an important role in the politics, economics and culture of Chang' an in the Tang Dynasty.

West Market was located in the southwest of imperial city (today between south Laodong Road and East Taoyuan Village), built in Sui Dynasty (A.D581-A.D.617), thrived in Tang Dynasty (A.D618-A.D.907), covered an area of 1600 mu, with construction area of more than 1 million square meters and more than 220 industries, which was flourished in Tang Dynasty. Chang' an of Tang dynasty practiced the fangshi pattern strictly, residential areas "fang" and economic zones "shi" did not interfere with each other, reflecting the social stratification and law social formation. East Market was the east third street of zhuque Avenue; West Market was the west third street of zhuque Avenue. West Market was surrounded by high walls, just like Lifang. Song Minqiu " Chang' an history" recoded, it had large scale, each "shi" accounted for about two "fang" area, there were four streets in it, and the walls were surrounded with 2 doors, which has been confirmed based on a comprehensive investigation and measurement. West Market was the most important market in China. It was a market that was for closed centralized trading, that is gathered similar goods, taking "shop" as the unit, with special management institutions

According to the results of archaeological excavations, West Market was rectangular, long from North to South 1031 meters, wide from East to West 927 meters, covering an area of 0.96 square kilometers. Today it is located in Xi' an City of east of East Taoyuan Village, west of Laomijia Bridge, south of China Aviation Supplies Holding Company northwest Co., Ltd. at the location of South Xianlao Market. It is found that 4-meter-wide wall base remains in the north and east during excavation work. There are two north-south streets and two east-west streets in the market. Four-lane streets crisscross the market. Then the whole market is divided into 9 rectangular areas. Two east-west streets are 327 meters apart; two north-south are 309 meters apart. Both sides of the street are provided with ditch. There is still 1-meter-wide pavement outside of the ditch.

Streets surround 9 areas of West Market, so it is convenient to trade. There are lanes in each area for easy access. Some discharge channel under the lane is connected to the ditch on both sides of the street. Commercial store sites all along the street shows that housing size is not large, face width 4 to 10 meters, depth 3 meters or so. The phenomenon of concentration of similar goods proves the existence of a certain type of shop. For instance, there are material beads, pearls, agate, crystal and other products in jewelry shop. Iron stores unearthed a number of iron nails, and small pieces of iron. West Market is far from Imperial Palace , instead surrounded by houses for the populace. So the market sell mostly clothing, candle, cake, medicine and other daily necessities. West Market is more prosperous than East Market. It is the main industrial and commercial areas and economic activity center of Chang' an City, and called as "Gold Market".

As the starting point of the Silk Road in Chang' an was close to West Market, a lot of foreign businessmen living around, West Market becomes an international trade market. The merchants from Central Asia, South Asia, Southeast Asia, Korea, Xinluo, Baekje, Japan and other countries assemble here, most of them live in "fangli" near West Market and East Market. So it is an exhibition place for various western and eastern goods and traders and merchants at home and abroad. These foreign merchants sell spices and drugs to Chinese Officers, and then buy jewelry, silk and porcelain from Chinese. There are many shops opened by foreign businessmen, such as Persian shops, jewelry shops, warehouses, and etc, including several pubs where many girls from the Western Regions dance and accompany in drinking. Li Bai' s poetry "The Juvenile" ever said " The juvenile stroll around the Gold Market", "laugh and walk into exotic pub".

Commercial trades of West Market expand west to Rome, east to Korea. West Market is the center of the world trade, fashion and entertainment, Cultural Exchange, with the biggest area, most developed format, and most extensive radiation. The prosperous market system and the strong economic foundation of West Market support Silk Road trading system. It is the starting point of the Silk Road in the true sense. As the way of commercial and cultural communication between the East and West, Silk Road make the Yellow River civilization, Ganges River civilization and the Mediterranean civilization collide and merge with each other, accelerate the development of the world economy and society, affect the process of human history and civilization. It can say that West Market is a window for the world to know Chang' an even China, also an important platform for Cultural exchange and trading. West Market' s prosperity reflects the opening of the Tang Dynasty and the prosperity of the trade, shows flourishing material civilization of the Great Tang.

中国官僚，再从中国买回珠宝、丝织品和瓷器等。西市中有许多外国商人开设的店铺，如波斯邸、珠宝店、货栈、酒肆等。其中还有许多西域姑娘为之歌舞侍酒的胡姬酒肆，时有少年光顾。李白的《少年行》就有“五陵少年金市东”，“笑入胡姬酒肆中”的诗句。

西市商业贸易西至罗马、东到高丽（今韩国和朝鲜），是占地面积最大、建筑面积最大、业态最发达、辐射面最广的世界贸易中心、时尚娱乐中心和文化交流中心。西市以其繁荣的市场体系、坚实的经济基础支撑着整个丝绸之路的贸易体系，是丝绸之路真正意义上的起点。丝绸之路作为东西方商贸与文化传播之路，使黄河文明、恒河文明和地中海文明相互碰撞和融合，加速了世界经济社会的发展，影响着人类历史文明的进程。可以说，作为丝路起点的西市，既是外部世界了解长安乃至中国的一个窗口，又是东西方文化交流、贸易往来的重要平台。西市的繁华，反射着唐朝开放的风气和繁荣的贸易，展现了大唐鼎盛发达的物质文明。

西向二街相距 327 米，南北向二相距 309 米，各街两侧均设有水沟，在水沟的外侧还发现有 1 米宽的人行道。

西市的 9 个区域四面均为街道，这样每个区域的周边都临街，便于交易。每个区域内还有便于内部通行的小巷，在有的巷道下还有砖砌的暗排水道与大街两侧的水沟相连。临街部分出土的商业店铺遗址表明，房屋的规模不大，面阔 4 至 10 米，进深 3 米多，均沿街毗连；而出土的同类物品相对集中的现象，也证明了某一类型店铺的存在，如珠宝商的店铺就多料珠、珍珠、玛瑙、水晶等制品，铁器店铺就出土了为数不少的铁钉、铁棍与小铁器残块等。而西市距三内较远，周围多平民百姓住宅，市场经营的商品，多是衣、烛、饼、药等日常生活品。西市商业较东市繁荣，是长安城的主要工商业区和经济活动中心，因此又被称之为“金市”。

西市距离唐长安丝绸之路的起点“开远门”较近，周围坊里住有不少外商，从而成为了一个国际性的贸易市场。这里有来自中亚、南亚、东南亚及高丽、百济、新罗、日本等各国各地区的商人，其中尤以中亚与波斯（今伊朗）、大食（今阿拉伯）的“胡商”最多，他们多侨居于西市或西市附近一些坊里。因此这里中外商贾云集，也是中外百货杂陈的东西方商品展销基地。这些外国的客商将带来的香料、药物卖给

苏武牧羊

Imprisonment of Su Wu

苏武牧羊
Imprisonment of Su Wu

苏武牧羊（公元前 140 年—前 60 年），字子卿，汉族，杜陵（今陕西西安）人，代郡太守苏建之子，西汉大臣。武帝时为郎。当时汉朝和匈奴的关系时好时坏，苏武奉命以中郎将身份持节出使匈奴，却被扣留。匈奴贵族多次威胁利诱，想要使其投降，苏武坚持不降，于是匈奴将他迁到北海（今贝加尔湖）边牧羊，扬言要公羊生子才可释放他回国。苏武历尽艰辛，留居匈奴十九年持节不屈，直到始元六年（公元前 81 年）才获释回汉。苏武去世后，汉宣帝将其列为麒麟阁十一功臣之一，彰显其节操。这就是历史上著名的"苏武牧羊"。

天汉元年（公元前 100 年），匈奴政权新单于即位，尊大汉为丈人，汉武帝为了表示友好，便派遣苏武率领一百多人出使匈奴，持旄节护送扣留在汉的匈奴使者回国，顺便送给单于很丰厚的礼物，以答谢单于。不料，就在苏武完成了出使任务，准备返回自己的国家时，匈奴上层发生了内乱，苏武一行受到牵连，被扣留下来，并被要求背叛汉朝，臣服单于。单于方面派卫律向苏武游说，许其丰厚的奉禄和高官，对苏武威逼利诱，软硬兼施，苏武却始终不为所动。匈奴见劝说没有用，就决定用酷刑。当时正值严冬，天上下着鹅毛大雪。单于命人把苏武关进一个露天的大地穴，断绝提供食品和水，希望这样可以改变苏武的信念。时间一天天过去，苏武在地窖里受尽了折磨。渴了，他就吃一把雪，饿了，就嚼身上穿的羊皮袄，冷了，就缩在角里与皮袄取暖。过了好些天，单于见濒临死亡的苏武仍然没有屈服的表示，只好把苏武放出来了。单于知道怎样胁迫苏武投降都没有希望，但又越发敬重苏武的气节，不忍心将其杀害，于是决定把苏武流放到西伯利亚的贝加尔湖一带，让他去牧羊。临行前，单于召见苏武说："既然你不投降，那我就让你去放羊，什么时候这些羊生了羊羔，我就让你回到你的大汉去。"

与他的同伴分开后，苏武被流放到了人迹罕至的贝加尔湖边。他发现单于让他放的羊全都是公羊。在这里，单凭个人的能力是无论如何也逃不掉的。而唯一与苏武作伴的，是那根代表汉朝的使节和一小群羊。苏武每天拿着这根使节放羊，心想总有一天能够拿着回到自己的国家。由于没有供应粮食，苏武只能掘野鼠所储藏的果实吃。而那根汉朝使节，由于起居都拿着，时刻不离身，节上的毛已经全部脱落。武帝天汉二年（公元前 99 年），李陵投降匈奴，不敢访求苏武，后单于派李陵去北海，为苏武设酒宴和歌舞，劝其投降。面对昔日好友的劝说，苏武也毫不动摇，坚守着对大汉的忠诚。

苏武在贝加尔湖牧羊长达十九年之久。这些年当中，当初下了命令囚禁他的匈奴单于已经去世，汉武帝也已驾崩，武帝的儿子汉昭帝继任皇位。几年后，匈奴和汉朝达成和议。汉昭帝派出使者来到匈奴，要求放回苏武、常惠等人。匈奴骗使者说苏武已经死了。第二次，汉朝又派使者到匈奴去。常惠请求看守他的人员同他前往，夜晚见了汉使，原本地述说了这几年在匈奴的情况，并要求汉使对单于说：汉天子在上林苑中射猎，射得一只大雁，脚上系着帛书，上面说苏武等人在北海。汉使万分高兴，照常惠所说的话去责问单于。单于听了吓了一大跳，说："苏武的忠义感动飞鸟了！"他向使者道歉，答应一定送回苏武。昭帝始元六年（前 81 年）春，苏武回到长安。当初苏武出使时，随从的有一百多人，这次跟着他回来的只剩了常惠等几个人了；苏武出使时刚四十岁，在匈奴受难十九年，回到长安时已接近六十高龄。当时长安城的百姓都出门迎接，称赞他是个有气节的大丈夫。

苏武面对单于的威逼利诱毫不动摇，面对十九年的流放之苦毫不畏惧，始终保持着对大汉的忠贞，他高洁的情操和高尚的品德不仅为时人所敬重，也为后人所颂扬。李陵称赞苏武："今足下还归，扬名于匈奴，功显于汉室，虽古竹帛所载，丹青所画，何以过子卿！"班固也曾慨叹："使于四方，不辱君命，苏武有之矣。"

Su Wu (140B.C.-60B.C.), Han, was born in Duling, son of Su Jian, a minister in the West Han Dynasty. Han and Xiongnu maintained an in-and-out partnership at that time. Emperor Wu commissioned Su, then the deputy commander of the imperial guards, to serve as an ambassador to Xiongnu. The Huns noble detained Su Wu, threatened and bribed for many times to make him surrender, but he still hold out. Su Wu was moved to Beihai (now Lake Baikal), and was threatened that he would be released when the ram gave birth. He was in exile for 19 years. Despite of so many difficulties he had gone through, he did not give away. Su was released to Han until 81B.C. In gratitude to 11 key officials who served him well, Emperor Xuan had their portraits painted onto the main gallery of the main imperial palace, Su was one of them.

In 100B.C, there had been a new chanyu who came into power in Xiongnu, who had expressed interest in peace with Han. So Emperor Wu commissioned Su, the deputy commander of the imperial guards, to serve as an ambassador to Xiongnu. However, when Su was going to return to Han, a civil strife occurred in the Huns. And they were detained and forced to surrender. Chanyu sent Wei Lv to persuade Su with high position and handsome salary， but it didn' t work. Then Chanyu decided to try to torture him. In a cruel winter, Su Wu was shut in a large open-air cellar without food and drink. However, for several days, Su survived by consuming wool from his coat and the snow that fell into the cellar. Chanyu was further surprised and thought that the gods were protecting him. Chanyu then exiled him to Lake Baikal and ordered him to tend a flock of rams, telling him that he would be allowed to go home when the rams would give birth to lambs.

Separated from his companions, Su Wu was exiled to remote Lake Baikal. He found it was impossible to escape solely on personal ability. The only company was the root on behalf of the Han Dynasty envoy and a small flock of rams. He believed that he would return homeland one day. During exile, Chanyu sent Li Ling, who had surrendered to Xiongnu after being defeated on the battlefield in 99 B.C, to visit Su. He tried to convince Su to surrender, but Su refused.

Several years later, Han ambassadors inquired of Su' s fate. The Xiongnu government claimed that Su had long died. However, Su' s old assistant Zhang secretly informed the ambassadors of Su' s exile. The ambassador told Chanyu, Emperor Zhao had killed a migratory bird while hunting, and that a letter from Su seeking help was found on the bird' s foot. Surprised, Chanyu admitted that Su was in fact still alive, and allowed him to go home. In all, Su was in exile for 19 years. In 81B.C, Su Wu returned to Chang' an with a few of fellows. He was nearly sixty years old when he came back. At that time, the people of Chang' an were all meet him and praised him as an integrity man.

Faced with force and bribery, he never changed his mind. Faced with bitterness of exile, he never feared. He kept loyalty to Han Dynasty. Su was respected and praised for his noble character. Li Ling commended: you are famous both at home and abroad. It' s hard to express your noble personality quality! Ban Gu ever sighed: Su Wu has fulfilled his responsibility!

丽人行

Satire on Fair Ladies

《丽人行》是中国唐代诗人杜甫的作品。作为一首“旧瓶装新酒”的七言乐府诗，其诗题在汉代刘向《别录》中已有记载。但因其内容是直接针对当时的宰相杨国忠兄妹，不用古乐府借古喻今的惯例，所以中唐的元稹称其为“新乐府”，因此可以视为杜甫新题乐府中的例外。这首诗大约作于天宝十二载（公元753年）。此前一年，杨国忠官拜右丞相兼文部尚书，势倾朝野。《旧唐书・杨贵妃传》中也曾记载：“玄宗每年十月，幸华清宫，国忠姊妹五家扈从。每家为一队，着一色衣；五家合队，照映如百花之焕发。而遗钿坠舄，瑟瑟珠翠，璨瓓芳馥于路。而国忠私于虢国，而不避雄狐之刺；每入朝，或联镳方驾，不施帷幔。每三朝庆贺，五鼓待漏，靓妆盈巷，蜡炬如昼。”从历史上看，杨家兄妹骄纵荒淫的生活在当时已达到了无以复加的地步。《丽人行》通过描写杨氏兄妹曲江春游的情景，讽刺了其奢侈糜乱的生活，曲折地反映了君王的昏庸和时政的腐败，同时也从一个角度反映出了安史之乱前夕的社会现实。唐代自武后以来，外戚擅权已成为统治阶层中一种通常现象，他们形成了一个特殊的利益集团，引起了广大人民的强烈不满，这也是后来酿成安史之乱的主因。

丽人行

三月三日天气新，长安水边多丽人。
态浓意远淑且真，肌理细腻骨肉匀。
绣罗衣裳照暮春，蹙金孔雀银麒麟。
头上何所有？翠微匐叶垂鬓唇。
背后何所见？珠压腰衱稳称身。
就中云幕椒房亲，赐名大国虢与秦。
紫驼之峰出翠釜，水晶之盘行素鳞。
犀箸厌饫久未下，鸾刀缕切空纷纶。
黄门飞鞚不动尘，御厨络绎送八珍。
箫鼓哀吟感鬼神，宾从杂遝实要津。
后来鞍马何逡巡，当轩下马入锦茵。
杨花雪落覆白蘋，青鸟飞去衔红巾。
炙手可热势绝伦，慎莫近前丞相嗔！

《丽人行》在内容结构上可分为三段：先泛写上巳曲江水边踏青丽人之众多，以及她们意态之娴雅、体态之优美、衣着之华丽，引出主角杨氏姐妹的娇艳姿色；次写宴饮的豪华及所得的宠幸，肴馔讲究色、香、味和器皿的衬托，“紫驼之峰出翠釜，水精之盘行素鳞”，举出一二品名，配以适当颜色，便写出了器皿的雅致，肴馔的精美丰盛以及其香、其味来，这么名贵的山珍海味，缕切纷纶而厌饫久未下箸，不须明说，三夫人的骄贵暴殄，已刻画无遗；最后写杨国忠的骄横，“杨花”二句似赋而实比兴，暗喻杨国忠与虢国夫人的淫乱，丞相权势煊赫、炙手可热，旁人近前却也嗔怒呵禁。整首诗场面宏大，鲜艳富丽，笔调细腻生动，讽刺含蓄不露。本是描写杨国忠兄妹，诗的开头却反从一般丽人写起，描绘其体貌服饰的华美，既是陪衬，又十分含蓄，继而笔锋一转，点出虢国夫人与秦国夫人，盛言排场的盛大、宴游的豪奢及趋炎附势者之众，见出杨氏兄妹的骄宠之态。诗人通篇只是写“丽人”们的生活情形，结尾两句，才算把主题点出，但依然不着议论，而是让读者自去批评。全诗语极铺排，富丽华美中蕴含清刚之气。虽然字面上不见讥刺痕迹，但在惟妙惟肖的描摹中，其隐含犀利的讥讽，已隐然入木三分。正如清人浦起龙《读杜心解》所评的，《丽人行》已经达到了“无一刺讥语，描摹处语语刺讥；无一慨叹声，点逗处声声慨叹”的艺术效果。

《丽人行》作为一篇成功的文学作品，其主题思想和倾向并不隐晦难懂，但作者并不明确指点出来，而是让这些从场面和情节中自然而然地流露出来。从头到尾，诗人都只是描写那些简短的场面和情节，采取像《陌上桑》那样一些乐府民歌中所惯常用的正面咏叹方式，态度严肃认真，笔触精工细腻，着色鲜艳富丽、金碧辉煌，丝毫不露油腔滑调，也不作漫画式的刻画。但令人惊叹不置的是，诗人就是在这一本正经的咏叹中，出色地完成了诗歌揭露腐朽、鞭挞邪恶的神圣使命，获得了比一般轻松的讽刺更为强烈的艺术批判力量。

"Satire on Fair Ladies" is the work of Du Fu, a great poet in Tang Dynasty. It is a seven-word musical palace poetry of "new wine in old bottles", whose title has been recorded in Liu Xiang' s "Bielu" of the Han Dynasty. Because the content is directly against the Prime Minister Yang Guozhong and his sister, it doesn' t use the conventions of ancient Yuefu, then it is called as "New Fu" by Yuan Zhen, a poet in Middle Tang. This poem was written about Tianbao twelve years (753 A.D.). The year before, Yang Guozhong had been appointed Prime Minister and had a great deal of power. "Book of Tang, Biography of Lady Yang" recorded, Emperor Xuanzong went to Huaqing Palac every October for short stays, five families of Yang Guozhong and his sisters followed. Each family composed a team, with uniform clothing; the big group of five families looked blooming and glowing. It was a very imposing procession of pretty faces and fine clothes, and the sweet scent filled the air. Yang Guozhong disobeyed Chinese old manners due to the secret affair with the lady of the Guo State. The first day of the first month, the servant would enter the Palace to pay their respects to the Emperor and the Empress. All of them dressed well, and the Palace were ablaze with candle. In history, Yang siblings lived a life of arrogant and dissolute to the extreme. "Satire on Fair Ladies" desicribed the scene of Yang siblings spring outing to satire their extravagant lifestyle, and exposed the dark reality before An-Shih Rebellion: fatuity corrupt rulers and social darkness. Since Empress Wu, Dukes feudal autocracy had been common phenomenon. The relative formed a special interest group, leading to strong dissatisfaction of the people. This was the main reason causing An-Shih Rebellion later.

Satire on Fair Ladies
The weather' s fine in the third moon on the third day,
By river side so many beauties in array.
Each of the ladies has a fascinating face,
Their skin is delicate, their manner full of grace.
Embroidered with peacocks and unicorns in gold,
Their dress in rich silks shines so bright when spring is old.
What do they wear on the head?
Emerald pendant leaves hang down in silver thread.
What do you see from behind?
How nice-fitting are their waistbands with peals combined.
Among them there' re the emperor' s favorite kin,
Ennobled Duchess of Guo comes with Duchess of Qin.
What do they eat?
The purple meat
Of camel' s hump cooked in green cauldron as a dish;
On crystal plate is served snow-white slices of raw fish.
See rhino chopsticks the satiated eaters stay,
And untouched morsels carved by belled knives on the tray.
When eunuchs' horses come running, no dust is raised;
They bring still more rare dishes delicious to the taste.

Listen to soul-stirring music of flutes and drums!
On the main road an official retinue comes.
A rider ambles on saddled horse, the last of all,
He alights, treads on satin carpet, enters the hall.
The willow down like snow falls on the duckweed white;
The blue bird picking red handkerchief goes in flight.
The prime minister' s powerful without a peer.
His angry touch would burn your hand. Do not come near!

The poetry can be divided into three sections based on content structure. Firstly, it says that many beautiful ladies are walking along Shangsi Qujiang. Their elegant semblance, graceful status and splendid dress set off the gorgeousness of Yang siblings. Secondly, the banquet is luxury; the cuisine is perfect in color, aroma and taste. "Of camel' s hump cooked in green cauldron as a dish; On crystal plate is served snow-white slices of raw fish." This sentence lists the names and colors of the vessels, converys fancy, excellence and value precious quite clearly and vividly. However, the ladies are so luxurious that leave the delicacies untouched. Finaly, Yang Guozhong is arrogant. The last two sentences imply the promiscuity between Yang guozhong and the lady of the Guo State. The Prime Minister covered a great power and became the hotshot at that time; common people were not permitted to approach him. The poetry is grand scenes, bright splendid, delicate strokes and euphemistic. The poetry begins from the description of common lady. Then, quite true, it extremely says the ostentation and extravagance for Mrs. Guo and Mrs. Qin. The poem just wrote common ladies' life in whole work, pointed the theme at the end of the poetry, leaving much space for the readers instead of any discussion. The language is not only magnificent but reveals a sense of fresh and muscular strength. Although the poem didn' t satire literally, his vivid character description was really penetrating. Just as Pu Qilong "DuDuXinJie" says, "Satire on Fair Ladies" has reached the artistic creation that no satire but irony contained in description. no sigh but emotion read between the lines.

As a successful literary work, "Satire on Fair Ladies" is not difficult to understand. But the poem chose to reveal the theme from the scene and the plot naturally instead of point it directly. He only described these short plot in the whole work, just like "By the Roadside Mulberry" , Yuefu songs of the Han Dynasty. The poetry is serious, bright splendid and delicate strokes. To our surprise, the poetry has accomplished the sacred mission of exposing the corruption and expanding the evil by singing seriously. And it has gained more powerful strength of culture criticism than easy irony.

丽人行 Satire on Fair Ladies

唐代扬州铜镜

Yangzhou Bronze Mirror of Tang

唐代扬州铜镜 Yangzhou Bronze Mirror of Tang

唐代扬州所在的长江中下游汉丹阳及其周边地区，自先秦以来就是重要的产铜区，到唐代更是当时五大采铜、冶铜区之一。根据文献记载，唐代铜铁的采造在矿产地设监进行，即对矿产就地加工，中央的掌冶署依仗的也是京畿附近的矿场。因此，由于地域上的优势，扬州成为了唐时铸镜的重要产区。

扬州上贡铜镜的时期，据旧籍记载为唐中宗到德宗时期，其中以开元、天宝时铸镜业最为繁荣。当时唐代两京地区不同阶段流行的镜类，在扬州几乎都有发现。而扬州铸镜中最精致的，是专为奉献给皇帝而特意加工的铜镜，有“方丈镜”、“江心镜”和“百炼镜”等。《异闻录》中记载，“唐天宝三载五月十五日，扬州进水心镜一面，纵横九寸，青莹耀日，背有盘龙长三尺四寸五分，势如生动，元（玄）宗览异之。”《朝野佥载》中也记载，“中宗令扬州造方丈镜，铸铜为桂树、金花银叶，帝每骑马自照，人马并在镜中。”所谓金花银叶系在镜背上，用胶漆贴以金、银薄片裁成的人物、花卉、虫兽之花样，再于上面髹漆数重之后细加研磨，直至金银片纹露于平面，这就是盛唐时期制作铜镜而工艺美术水平相当高的金银平脱法。解放后，扬州出土了许多唐镜，如“打马球菱花镜”、“海马葡萄纹镜”、“双狮纹方镜”等，其制作精良，一镜之上，有平面、凹面、凸面之分，照物成像，有大小、反正、远近之别，这也证明了唐代扬州铸镜已达到相当的高水平。

扬州出土的唐镜，从纹饰上看，主要可以归为两大类。第一类是动物植物纹饰镜。动物中既有飞禽，又有走兽，这些动物有取材于现实生活的，如鹦鹉、练鹊、孔雀、蝴蝶、蜻蜓，以及牛、鸡、河马、乌龟等，还有取材于神话的，如天马、鸾凤、天鹿、狻猊、龙等。植物纹饰，则以宝相花纹和葡萄花纹较多。这是唐代铜镜较为普遍的一种装饰纹样，唐代也沿用串枝莲卷叶花草等花纹来作为铜镜边缘的装饰，这继承了汉镜的特点，而纹饰之饱满，形态之逼真却又是唐镜的一个发展。第二类则是铭文和人物故事镜。铭文镜中，如卍字镜、千秋万岁镜、王典镜等别具一格。与此同时，唐朝佛教盛行，这在铜镜的纹饰上也有所反映，在莲花纹的基础上加以美化，创造了更加富丽的宝相花镜，就是其中一例。

根据文献的记载和专家的研究，唐代扬州的私营铸镜作坊以盈利为目的，这就意味着扬州铜镜在本国内有贸易流通。但中央或地方政府对民间技能工巧的匠人具有实际的控制力，可以直接驱使为其服务，或以官督民造的形式进行访求或索取式的生产。而当时的扬州铜镜不仅在中国范围内进行贸易，更是通往世界，进行着跨域的商贸活动。丝路物语，镜无不据。1998 年，德国一家打捞公司在印尼海域的一块黑色大礁岩附近发现一艘唐代沉船，名为“黑石”号。船只装载着经由东南亚运往西亚、北非的中国文物，有瓷器、金银器、钱币、铜镜等文物 67000 多件。由于扬州在唐代是“陆上丝绸之路”与“海上丝绸之路”的交汇点，于是在当时，大食、波斯等国商人从国外带来了珠宝、香料、药材，又从扬州运回瓷器、铜镜等中国特产，这就使得扬州铜镜走出了中国，走向了世界。在扬州输出到西域等国家的“出口”铜镜中，有的背面还绘上了葡萄、海马这样的异域元素，考虑到的就是西方人的审美需求。

唐代扬州铜镜制作精良，造型优美，纹饰精致，在当时颇有盛名。因此，扬州铜镜不仅在本国内进行流通，同时也被作为进献帝王的贡品。并且，扬州作为水陆交通的枢纽，也是对外贸易的重要商埠，以经济繁华和文化发达著名于世，这就使得扬州铜镜有了走向世界的良好条件。由于兼具审美和使用价值，因此在当时的通商贸易当中，铜镜与瓷器一样，作为中国的特产，在西域商人中十分受欢迎。扬州铜镜承载着中国古代精湛的制作技艺和优秀的传统文化，为古代中国与世界各国的文化交流起到了一定的作用。

Yangzhou and its surrounding regions have been the main area to produce bronze since pre-Qin. And it became more important in Tang Dynasty. According to the historical document, peoples of the Tang Dynasty exploited and processed the mineral resources in same place. Therefore, due to the geographical advantages, Yangzhou became an important producing area of bronze mirror in Tang Dynasty.

Casting mirror industry was the most prosperous in Kaiyuan and Tianbao. At that time, popular mirrors of two different stages almost have been found in Yangzhou. The most exquisite was specially designed for the emperor, such as "Fangzhang mirror", "Jiangxin mirror", "Bailian mirror" and so on. "Abnormal smell" recorded: in 15th may, 744, a Shuixinjing was tribute, measuring 27cm in diameter. There was a vivid coiled dragon on the back of mirror. Emperor Xuanzong was surprised about it. "Chaoyeqianzai" also recorded: Emperor Zhongzong ordered to produce "fangzhang mirror". When he was riding, he would see the horse and himself in the mirror. After liberation, Yangzhou unearthed a lot of Tang mirrors. They were all magnificent and delicate in production. It is proved that the technology of casting mirror of Yangzhou has reached a very high level in Tang Dynasty.

The mirror unearthed in Yangzhou, according to the pattern may divide into two big kinds. The first type was decorated by the patterns of animals and plants. Some of the animals were based on real life, such as parrots, long-tailed flycatcher, peacocks, butterflies, dragonflies, cow, chicken, horse, turtle and so on. Others were based on myths, such as Pegasus, phoenix, fairy deer, lion and dragon and so on. The Tang Dynasty also followed Han's tradition of decorating a string of branch lotus leaf as the edge of the mirror. And the full decorative patterns and realistic form ware new development of Tang mirror. The second type was mirrors with inscriptions and stories. Meanwhile, Buddhism prevailed in Tang Dynasty, which also reflected in the patterns of mirrors.

According to the literature and experts, private workshops in Yangzhou produced bronze mirror for profit in Tang Dynasty. It means that Yangzhou bronze mirror has traded in the domestic. However, the governments have controlled folk craftsmen. They drove the men work for them. Yangzhou bronze mirror was not only traded in China, but went to the world. In 1998, a German fishing company found a shipwreck of the Tang dynasty in Indonesia, called as "black stone". The Ship carrying Chinese cultural relics through Southeast Asia to West Asia and North Africa, more than 67000 pieces of porcelain, such as gold and silver wares, coins, bronze mirrors and other artifacts. Yangzhou was the junction of land Silk Road and marine Silk Road. Arab, Persian businessmen brought jewelry, spices, herbs, from abroad, and went back with porcelain, bronze mirrors and other Chinese specialty from Yangzhou. So Yangzhou bronze mirror went out of China and went to the world. Considering the aesthetic demand of the West, some export mirrors were painted with exotic elements such as grapes and hippocampus.

Yangzhou bronze mirror was well produced, elegant with exquisite ornamentation. It was quite famous in Tang Dynasty. Therefore, it was not only in the domestic circulation, also presented to the Emperor. Yangzhou is famous for its economic prosperity and cultural development. It is convenient for Yangzhou bronze mirrors to trade in the world. Like china, Yangzhou bronze mirrors were quite popular among the businessmen of the Western Regimes. So it has played an important role in the cultural communication between the ancient China and the world.

图书在版编目（CIP）数据

大唐丝路盛景图 / 吴铭峰编 . -- 上海 : 交通大学出版社 , 2016.09

ISBN 978-7-313-14743-9

Ⅰ . ①大… Ⅱ . ①吴… Ⅲ . ①画集 – 中国 – 现代 Ⅳ . ① I216.2

中国版本图书馆 CIP 数据核字 (2016) 第 259786 号

大唐丝路盛景图

主编：吴铭峰

绘画：雒建安、邓先荷

出版发行：上海交通大学出版社 SHANGHAI JIAO TONG UNIVERSITY PRESS

地址：上海市番禺路 951 号　邮政编码：200030

电话：021-64071205

出版人：韩建民

印制：上海盛隆印务有限公司

经销：全国新华书店

开本：8 开

印张：14.5

字数：15 万

版次：2016 年 9 月第一版　印次：2016 年 9 月第一次印刷

书号：ISBN 978-7-313-14743-9

定价：600 元（一函两册）